大為和海琳在中國

大為和海琳在中國

# 大為 和海琳在中國

## 中 級 漢 語 教 材

# David And Helen In China

## Part I

Phyllis Ni Zhang  張霓

with

Yuan-yuan Meng  孟苑苑
Donald K. Chang  張光誠
Irene C. Liu  劉瑞年

Far Eastern Publications
Yale University

This is an **FEP** book.

Copyright © 1999 by Phyllis N. Zhang

Telephone: (203) 432 3109
Fax: (203) 432 3111
E-mail: john.montanaro@yale.edu
Web site: http//www.yale.edu/fep

Library of Congress Cataloging in Publications data:
**DAVID AND HELEN IN CHINA: An Intermediate Chinese Course,
Part One and Part Two (bound separately; sold as set only)
(traditional character edition)
Phyllis N. Zhang with Yuann-yuann Meng, Donald K. Chang and
Irene C. Liu**
1. Chinese language
2. Chinese language: post-basic, for foreign speakers, English
3. High School and College I. Title
1999

**ISBN 088710-190-9**

Publisher: Far Eastern Publications, Yale University, New Haven, CT
Managing Editor: John S. Montanaro
Design: Forsyth Computer Services
Illustrations: Huiming Xiong, Kunwu Li and others
Printed in the United States of America by McNaughton and Gunn
Company, Saline, MI

10 9 8 7 6 5 4 3 2
First Printing, July, 1999
Second Printing, July, 2003

# 大衛 和海琳在中國

中 級 漢 語 教 材

David  And  Helen  In  China

# Acknowledgments

Support for this textbook project came in part from the Consortium for Language Teaching and Learning. Their financial support made completion of this book much easier. I am grateful also to the Department of East Asian Languages and Cultures at Columbia University for providing me with a multitude of opportunities to experiment with this textbook in an actual classroom teaching situation. Further, I am indebted to my colleagues Ling Mu and Zhengguo Kang from Yale University as well as my fellow-teachers at Columbia, for their valuable comments and suggestions. I especially would like to thank my Columbia coworkers, Yuanyuan Meng for her substantive contributions, and Donald Chang and Irene Liu for their generous assistance in completing some sections of the book.

I also wish to extend my gratitude to Ann Huss, Helen Raffel and John S. Montanaro for their assistance in editing and proofing the English text, and to the Chinese artists, Huiming Xiong, Kunwu Li, Jianhua Li, Shek Cheung, and my student, Rainne Wu, for their help with the illustrations and artwork. Finally, participants in my intermediate Chinese classes at Columbia--too numerous to be listed here, are remembered for their helpful comments.

While each person's contribution is individually appreciated, I alone am responsible for the ideas, opinions, and deficiencies in the final version.

Phyllis Zhang
July, 2003 (2nd Edition)

# 大為和海琳在中國

## 目錄 (Contents)

# Introduction

*David and Helen in China: An Intermediate Chinese Course,* Parts I and II, is designed for college classes or self-study of Chinese as a foreign language. It is available in traditional **or** simplified character editions. The course assumes that the learner is already familiar with 600 to 800 vocabulary items as well as the basic sentence structures of modern Mandarin usually introduced in a beginning level course. These materials can be used for a yearlong course at the college level or for an intensive summer course (assuming eight to nine weeks duration and eight to nine teaching hours for each lesson). It has been designed so that it can follow completion of a number of popular elementary texts, such as, *Colloquial Chinese* by T'ung and Pollard, *Chinese Primer* by D.T. Chen, et al., *Practical Chinese Reader* by Liu Xun, et al, or *Integrated Chinese* by T. C.Yao, et al. In this newest printing of July, 2003, typos and other errors not caught in the original 1999 edition have been corrected. In addition, some exercises have been revised.

This intermediate course, with its accompanying audio program, aims at expanding the learner's ability to handle everyday situations and tasks in Chinese. The lessons are presented in the form of a narrative story, with dialogue, which describe the experiences of two fictionalized college students, David and Helen, in Beijing and Taipei, respectively. In addition to introducing specific language forms, the content of the first half of the course, (Part I, Lessons 1-9) focuses on such everyday tasks as shopping, writing a letter, making a phone call, renting a room, or looking for a job, **etc**. The second half (Part II, Lessons 10-18) presents more culture-related topics, including Chinese social norms for politeness, Chinese holidays, traditional notions of love and marriage, and Chinese myths, etc. Language usage in Part II gradually shifts from informal to semiformal style towards the end of the book, covering speech commonly used in business settings as well as in social settings.

**Components of Each Lesson**

1. **Text:** narrates the continuous story in Chinese characters, usually consisting of a narrative and a dialog. (Created by P. Zhang)
2. **Vocabulary:** lists new words in the order in which they appear in the Text on pages facing the relevant text. (Prepared by D. Chang)
3. **Notes:** explains difficult points in the Text. (Written by P. Zhang)
4. **Focusing on Structure:** presents grammatical features exemplified in the Text with explanations and examples. (Written by P. Zhang)
5. **Word Usage:** provides typical examples and idiomatic usage of new words; listed by grammatical categories. (Prepared by Y. Meng)
6. **Sentence Patterns and Expressions:** provides sample sentences illustrating grammar points raised in the Text, occasionally accompanied by English translations to facilitate understanding. (Prepared by Y. Meng)
7. **Learning about Culture:** introduces cultural information related to the lesson's topic. ( Written by I. Liu and P. Zhang; edited by John S. Montanaro)
8. **Listening Comprehension: presents** follow-up-aural exercises based on the new words and patterns. Section I **focuses on sentence level activities** while Section II aims at paragraph-level discourse. (Script and exercises created by Y. Meng)
9. **Exercises:**
   - <u>Vocabulary Exercises</u> concentrates on specific vocabulary words and usage patterns for the new vocabulary items of each lesson. (Designed by P. Zhang and I. Liu)

- Sentence Patterns and Grammar Exercises are written exercises to practice the sentence patterns and expressions and important structural features of each lesson. (Designed by P. Zhang)

- Reading Comprehension Exercises serves several purposes: (1) to review known vocabulary and introduce related new words, (2) to reinforce newly-learned vocabulary and patterns in various contexts, (3) to improve reading skills and speed while developing problem-solving ability through the use of a dictionary. The reading passages also stimulate discussion and generate writing activities. They are occasionally reinforced with authentic materials. (Created by P. Zhang)

- Speaking Tasks often consist of two parts: mini-talks or short exchanges and paragraph-level communicative tasks. The mini-talks/short exchanges focus on practicing appropriate use of speech patterns and responses, while the paragraph-level activities involve situational conversations or communicative tasks providing opportunities to develop communication skills in a particular setting. In most cases pictures and sketches are used to stimulate spoken language. (Designed by P. Zhang)

- Writing Tasks are designed to motivate the learner to use language for writing and to practice new words and expressions while reviewing already-introduced features of language. The writing tasks are often derived from or are related to the Reading or Speaking Tasks and provide the learner with additional opportunities to do further work or to deepen understanding of a topic. (Designed by P. Zhang)

10. **Audio Program:** provides a recording of each lesson's (a) the vocabulary and text, (b) word usage and sentence patterns, and (c) the listening comprehension exercises. The Audio Program on CD (MP3) is available packaged with the two volume set or separately. The audio program is also available in cassette format.

In addition each volume includes the following appendices (Prepared in part by D. Chang):

A. **Character Writing Guides**: presents characters selected from the new words in each lesson for writing practice.

B. **Sentence Patterns and Expressions Index:** lists (for Part One) the sentence patterns and expressions introduced in lessons 1-9 for quick reference and review. Part Two contains a complete index of all patterns and expressions (Lessons 1-18), arranged alphabetically with examples and lesson references.

C. **Vocabulary Glossary:** lists all new words introduced in the main text of each volume. Part II contains a complete glossary of vocabulary from the main text of Lessons 1-18, arranged alphabetically by *pinyin*-spelling with Chinese characters and lesson references.

### *Pinyin* Spellings and Grammar Terms Used in the Textbook:

The *pinyin* spellings used in the text are based largely on the Dictionary of Modern Chinese (*Xiandai Hanyu Cidian*, Commercial Press, Hong Kong, 1996). A double slash (//) is used in separable disyllabic or polysyllabic verbs such as verb-objects or resultative verb compounds, indicating that other elements may be inserted.

Some of the grammar discussed in the book derives from my own research as well as from observations of other Chinese and Western linguists, including, Yuen Ren Chao, James H-Y Tai, Charles N. Li, Sandra A. Thompson, and Simon Dik, among others. Grammatical terms, such as the ones used for parts of speech, mostly follow the conventions used in the text, *Speak Mandarin*, by Fenn and Tewksbury, Yale University Press, New Haven, 1967.

Phyllis Zhang
New York, 2003

# 詞類縮語表
## Abbreviations of Parts of Speech

A:      adverb (e.g.,他<u>真</u>聰明；我<u>也</u>去；你們<u>一塊兒</u>説。)

Adj.:      adjective (e.g.,<u>大</u>孩子，<u>好</u>學生,or as Predicate, e.g., 我們都<u>好</u>，可是很<u>忙</u>。)

AV:      auxiliary verb (e.g.,她真<u>會</u>説話；我不<u>喜歡</u>唱歌。)

BF:      bound form (character not to be used by itself; e.g., 你<u>們</u>；<u>右</u>手；<u>南</u>邊)

CV:      co-verb (e.g., 我<u>跟</u>你們説中文；老師<u>對</u>我們很客氣。)

EV:      equative verb (e.g.,那個人<u>是</u>我哥哥；你<u>姓</u>什麼？)

IE:      idiomatic expression (e.g., "<u>沒關係！</u>"；"<u>不敢當</u>"；"<u>哪裡，哪裡！</u>")

Interj:      interjection (e.g.,<u>啊</u>！你來了；<u>哎呀</u>，我忘了。)

M:      measure word (e.g., 五<u>個</u>星期；好幾<u>張</u>紙；十多<u>封</u>信)

MA:      movable adverb (e.g., 我<u>雖然</u>會説，<u>可是</u>説得不太好。)

N:      noun (e.g.,<u>桌子</u>；<u>父母</u>；<u>衣服</u>；<u>咖啡</u>；<u>意思</u>)

Nu:      number (e.g.,<u>六</u>；<u>八百</u>；<u>兩千</u>多；<u>四十幾</u>個人)

P:      particle (e.g., 你好<u>嗎</u>？；他怎麼還沒來<u>呢</u>？；這孩子好高<u>呀</u>！)

PH:      phrase (e.g., <u>一路平安</u>；<u>好久不見</u>)

Pref:      prefix (word used as the beginning of a compound; e.g.,<u>男</u>人；<u>公共</u>汽車)

PW:      place word (e.g., <u>這裡</u>；<u>那兒</u>；<u>地方</u>；<u>北京</u>；<u>美國</u>)

QW:      question word (e.g., <u>什麼</u>？<u>怎麼</u>？<u>誰</u>？<u>為什麼</u>？<u>哪個</u>？)

RV:      resultative verb compound (e.g.,<u>看見</u>；<u>睡着</u>；<u>找到</u>；<u>搬出去</u>)

RVE:      resultative verb ending (e.g., 看<u>懂</u>；睡<u>着</u>；找<u>到</u>；拿<u>上去</u>)

SP:      specifier (e.g.,<u>這</u>個人；<u>那</u>本書；<u>每</u>個國家；<u>頭</u>兩年)

Suf:      suffix (used as word ending; e.g., 我<u>們</u>；月<u>底</u>；錄音<u>機</u>)

TW:      time word (e.g., <u>今天</u>；<u>上午九點</u>；<u>下禮拜</u>；<u>一九九五年</u>)

V:      verb (with or without object; e.g.,<u>來</u>；<u>打</u>；<u>買</u>；<u>知道</u>；<u>玩兒</u>；<u>教</u>)

VO:      verb-object compound (e.g., <u>吃飯</u>；<u>説話</u>；<u>寫字</u>；<u>走路</u>；<u>做事</u>)

VP:      verbal phrase (part of a sentence; usually without subject; e.g.,<u>作三頓飯</u>；<u>在這裡住</u>)

<u>Other Abbreviations used</u>

colloq: colloqial; used often in conversation      lit: literary; used often in writing or refined speech

re: refering to      sb.:somebody      sth.: something      syn.:synonym

# "你會想我嗎？"

## ― 出國以前 ―

第一課

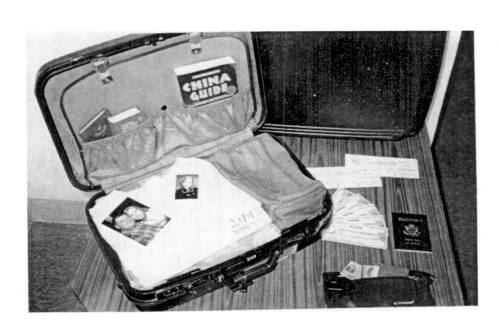

| Situation | Structure | Culture |
|-----------|-----------|---------|
| 語言情景 | 語言結構 | 文化介紹 |

In this lesson you'll meet David and Helen for the first time as both prepare for their trips and say goodbye to each other.

You'll focus on these new structures:
- 會 and 要 to express the future;
- making your language vivid with reduplicated adjectives.

You'll learn about cultural practices when Chinese go off on a long journey.

# "你會想我嗎？"
## --出國以前--

　　李大爲和他的女朋友吳海琳這幾天興奮得不得了，因爲他們就要出國了。 大爲要到北京去留學，海琳要到台北去看親戚。這幾天來他們都在做出國準備：申請護照和簽證、買飛機票、收拾行李等等，忙得團團轉。再過兩天，他們就要分別坐飛機到北京和台北去了。

　　大爲是美國人，原名叫 David Leigh，"李大爲"是他的中文名字。他是在美國西部生的，在東部長大的。海琳是華裔美國人，是十多年前跟父母從台灣移民到美國來的。大爲和海琳是一年前在大學裡認識的。那時大爲剛開始學中文，想找一個中國人練習口語。海琳的中文說得很不錯，當時[i]在上高級中文班，很願意幫大爲的忙，這樣他們就認識了。爲了幫助大爲說好中文，海琳跟大爲約好他們在一起的時候只說中文，不說英文。開始的時候大爲覺得很不自然，可是練習了一段時間以後，也就習慣了。

　　這一年來大爲和海琳常常在一起，成了好朋友。大爲越來越喜歡海琳，如果幾天沒看見她，就會覺得 少了點什麼。海琳也覺得沒有大爲，生活一定會很沒有意思，所以這一次分別對他們兩個人來說都有點不習慣。這一天他們在一起吃飯告別。

---

i. 當時 (at that very time; at the time in question) is similar to 那時 in meaning. 當天 ("that very/same day"), 當晚 ("that very/same night"), are similar forms.

| | | | |
|---|---|---|---|
| 會 | 会 | huì | AV will/would, may/might, be likely |
| 李大爲 | 李大为 | Lǐ Dàwéi | N (Chinese name of) David Leigh |
| 吳海琳 | 吴海琳 | Wú Hǎilín | N (Chinese name of) Helen Wu |
| 興奮 | 兴奋 | xīngfèn | ADJ/N excited, thrilled; excitement |
| 留學 | 留学 | liúxué | VO to study abroad |
| 親戚 | 亲戚 | qīnqi | N relatives (of extended family) |
| 準備 | 准备 | zhǔnbèi | V/N to prepare; preparation |
| 申請 | 申请 | shēnqǐng | V/N to apply (for); application |
| 護照 | 护照 | hùzhào | N passport |
| 簽證 | 签证 | qiānzhèng | N visa |
| 飛機 | 飞机 | fēijī | N airplane |
| 票 | | piào | N ticket |
| 收拾 | | shōushi | V to put (things) in order, tidy up |
| 團團轉 | 团团转 | tuántuán zhuàn | ADJ (so busy that you) run around in circles |
| 分別 | | fēnbié | V/N/A to separate; separation; separately, respectively |
| -部 | | bù | BF area, region (as PW Suffix) |
| 西部 | | xībù | N the west; western part |
| -裔 | | yì | BF of descent |
| 華裔 | 华裔 | Huáyì | N foreign citizen of Chinese origin |
| 移民 | | yímín | V/N to immigrate/emigrate; immigrant/emigrant |
| -語 | -语 | yǔ | BF language, speech (used as N-suf) |
| 口語 | 口语 | kǒuyǔ | N spoken language |
| 當時 | 当时 | dāngshí | TW at that time, then, at that very moment |
| -級 | -级 | jí | BF level, rank |
| 高級 | 高级 | gāojí | ADJ high-level/rank, advanced, advanced level |
| 幫助 | 帮助 | bāngzhù | V/N to assist, help; assistance |
| 約 | 约 | yuē | V to make an appointment |
| 約好 | 约好 | yuēhǎo | RV to fix time/place, etc. for a meeting |
| 自然 | | zìrán | ADJ/A natural; naturally |
| 段 | | duàn | M section, part |
| 習慣 | 习惯 | xíguàn | V/N to get used to; habit |
| 成 | | chéng | V to turn into, become |
| 少 | | shǎo | V to lack, be short of |
| 告別 | | gàobié | VO/N to bid farewell, say goodbye; farewell |

大爲：海琳——

海琳：嗯？[ii]

大爲：我想問問你——我們分別以後，你會不會想我？

海琳：那還用說嗎？當然會了！而且我會——

大爲：想我想得吃不下飯？睡不着覺？

海琳：不對！我會——哈哈大笑！

大爲：什麼？哈哈大笑？！爲什麼？

海琳：因爲我想你的時候，就會想起[iii]

我們第一次見面的時候你那種——那種傻傻的[iv]樣子，真好笑！

大爲：你當時的樣子才真的好笑呢[v]，有點——怪怪的！

海琳：好了好了[vi]，不跟你開玩笑了。你到了北京，別忘了給我寫信。

大爲：放心，忘不了。

海琳：好，祝你一路順風！

大爲：也祝你一路順風！

ii. 嗯 (ng) (interjection) corresponds to English "Yes?", "What?", "Oh?", "Huh?"

iii. 想起(來) (resultative compound verb) means "remember", "recall" or "be reminded of." Distinguish it from 想 ("think","think about", "think of"; "miss"). Contrast:

　　我在想一件事。 I am thinking about something.

　　我想起(來)一件事。 (That) reminded me of something/I've thought of something (as a result of something said, done, etc.)

iv. 傻傻的，怪怪的 are reduplicated adjectives. Saying the adjective twice makes the resulting expression more vivid. See Structural Notes for more on this feature.

v. "你當時的樣子才真的好笑呢。" (*You* actually had a funny look then. (Not me!) 才.....呢 corresponds to English expression in refuting "you're (I'm, he's etc.) the one who (was/did that) - - not me!"

　　他唱得才好呢。 She actually sings better (than somebody else we know about).

　　真的 (really; indeed) is used to confirm a fact or add an emphasis to a statement. It can be shorted to 真 sometimes. However there is a real difference between 真的 and 真 followed by an adjective or stative verb (e.g. 好) or a verb (e.g. 喜歡) because 真 conveys an emotive tone. Compare:

　　他真的唱得很好。 She really does sing nice. (adds confirmation)

　　他唱得真好！ She sings nicely. (description with admiration)

vi. 好了好了 corresponds to "Alright, alright", "That's enough", or "Stop it". Similar forms include 行了行了 or 得了得了.

| | | | |
|---|---|---|---|
| 而且 | | érqiě | MA moreover, and also |
| 哈哈 | | hāhā | ON Ha, ha! |
| 見面 | 见面 | jiàn//miàn | VO to meet (someone), see |
| 種 | 种 | zhǒng | M type, kind |
| 傻 | | shǎ | ADJ silly, foolish |
| 樣子 | 样子 | yàngzi | N appearance, look |
| 好笑 | | hǎoxiào | ADJ be funny, amusing |
| 放心 | | fàng//xīn | VO/SV to rest assured, feel relieved |
| 祝 | | zhù | V to wish (as in "I wish you luck") |
| 一路順風 | 一路顺风 | yílù shùnfēng | PH "Bon voyage!" "Have a nice trip!" |

判斷出以下詞語的意思：
(Figure out the meaning of the following)

出國　　　　　（出国）
西部
原名
大笑
高級中文班　　（高级中文班）
收拾行李

回答問題：

1.李大爲和吳海琳是哪國人？他們都是在美國生的嗎？
2.大爲和海琳是怎麼認識的？
3.他們爲什麼這幾天很興奮？他們都在做什麼？
4.爲什麼他們這次分別有點不習慣？
5.海琳是不是覺得大爲很傻？
6.你跟你的好朋友告別的時候，你會說什麼？

# 語言結構
## Focusing on Structure

## I. Using "會", "要" To Express the Future

會, in addition to meaning "can" or "know how to", that is, learned ability, (我會開車), when followed by a verb or adjective (stative verb), also conveys future tense, especially in the sense of 'confident prediction' or likelihood. It also implies plan or intention under certain circumstances. 會 can also express one's planned action. English translation runs to words like "will"/ "would", "may"/"might", etc. 的 is sometimes used at the end of the clause to add an assuring tone (是 會...的).

**Examples:**
- 你會想我嗎？ Will you miss me?
- 他今天（是）不會在家（的）。 He will not/won't be at home today. (prediction)
- 他今天可能不會在家。 He may not (probably won't) be at home today. (likelihood)
- 如果我去中國，我就會去找他。 If I go to China, I'll go see him. (intention)
- 如果我去中國，我一定會去找他。 If I go to China, I'll definitely go see him. (plan/intention)
- 你放心，我是不會把那件事告訴他（的）。 Don't worry. I won't tell him about it. (responsive promise)
- 她看見你一定會很高興的。 She will certainly be happy when she sees you. (prediction)
- 你到了北京會有人在那兒等你的。 Someone will meet you there when you arrive in Beijing. (planned action)

要, when followed by an action verb often expresses determination or desire to do something. Typically the action is certain or scheduled.

**Examples:**
- 我今天要到學校去。 I'll go to school today. --(as originally scheduled)
- 我去中國的時候要去找他。 I'm going to visit him when I'm in China. --(determination)
- 他要把這件事告訴你。 He is going to tell you about this. --(determination)

*Note that 想 (not 要) is used to express one's wish to do something without certainty of realization ("want to/ would like to..."). In this case an adverb of degree (like 很) can precede 想. 想 (short for 想要) may also be used to politely express desire.*
**Examples:**
- 我很想去中國。 I really want to go to China. ( But maybe I won't be able to go) (Incorrect: 我很要去中國。 )
- 我想喝點茶。 I'd like to have some tea. (Polite request said to your host.)

## II. Making Language Vivid with Reduplication: Saying the Adjective Twice (I)

Adjectives (sometimes called Stative Verbs), when reduplicated, express a vividness not conveyed in the plain form. The reduplicated form can describe <u>physical appearance or features, conditions, manners or attitude</u> and can stand alone with 的, or can modify a following noun.

**Examples:**
- 你那種傻傻的樣子，真好笑。
- 她的眼睛大大的，嘴小小的，中國人覺得很好看。
- 我把你的名字寫得大大的，他一定看得見。

# 辭彙用法
## Word Usage

### Verbs
- 申請：申請學校；申請工作；申請護照；申請簽證；申請移民到美國來。
- 收拾：收拾行李；收拾房間；收拾屋子；行李收拾好了。/他把屋子收拾得很乾淨。
- 過：時間過得真快！/過了五分鐘車還沒開。/過兩天他就要走了。
- 坐：坐飛機；坐車；坐地鐵；坐過一次飛機；從來沒坐過飛機；坐了十六個鐘頭的飛機
- 開始：開始學中文；開始上第二課；電影開始了。/學校明天開始上課。
- 練習：練習口語；練習說中文；練習得不夠；多練習幾次；做<u>練習</u>(N)。
- 幫助：幫助他學中文；幫助他收拾行李；他幫助過我很多次。
- 學習：學習中文；學習開車；他喜歡學習，不喜歡玩。/他的<u>學習</u>(N)很好。
- 生：你是在哪兒生的？/她是一九七三年生的。/她生了一個女兒。
- 忘：忘了買東西；忘了你的名字；別把那件事忘了。/我忘不了(liǎo)他。
- 分別：分別了十年；這一次分別對我們來說很不容易。/
  Adv:我<u>分別</u>給他們寫了一封信。/他和他太太要<u>分別</u>坐車來。
- 習慣：不習慣美國的生活；不習慣說中文；不習慣跟他分別很長時間。

### Verb-Object Compounds
- 出國：出國留學；出過兩次國；經常出國；沒出過國
- 留學：到美國去留學；留過兩次學；我從中國到這裡來留學，我是中國<u>留學生</u>(Mod)。
- 做準備：做出國準備；做考試準備；做了幾天準備；沒做好準備。
- 告別：跟親戚朋友告別；我們是在學校裡告別的。
- 睡覺：睡午覺；睡不着覺；睡了一大覺；昨天(睡覺)睡得太晚，所以沒睡夠。
- 見面：跟他見面；見過一次面；沒見過面；不常見面；我們兩年沒見面了。
- 開玩笑：我跟他開了一個玩笑。/我現在要工作，別跟我開玩笑。
- 放心：他做事我不放心。/你放心吧，這件事不會有問題的。

### Resultative Verb Compounds
- 約好：我跟他約好明天去看電影。/我跟他約好三點鐘在圖書館見面。/ 我們沒約好去哪兒。
- 長大：你是在哪兒長大的？/他現在長得多大了？/這種狗長不大。

### Nouns
- 生活：我的生活過得很舒服。/這裡的生活很沒意思。/我不習慣這裡的生活。
- 樣子：人的樣子；書的樣子；衣服的樣子；他的樣子很奇怪。/他的樣子很像中國人。

### Others
- 不得了：累得不得了；貴得不得了；高興得不得了；興奮得不得了
- 華-：華裔美國人；華僑 (huáqiáo: overseas Chinese)；華人；華語

# 句型和習慣用語
## Sentence Patterns and Expressions

**1. (time expression)(以)來 ......  (during/over the past [days/months,etc.],... )**

- 這一個月（以）來，我看了不少書。I have read quite a few books during the past month.
- 這一年（以）來，他們常常在一起，成了好朋友。

**Complete:**

- 這幾天以來，_____

**Translate:**

- I have become acquainted with many new friends over the past six months.


**2. 這(time expression)(以)來， Sb.都在 V... ( Sb. has been doing sth. for the past... )**

- 這一個月來，他都在做出國準備。
  He has been making preparations to go abroad for the past month.
- 這幾天來，我都在念書，準備下個星期的考試。

**Complete:**

- 甲：這半年來，你都在忙些什麼？
- 乙：_____

**Translate:**

- He has been practicing speaking Chinese for the past three months.


**3. Adj. / V 得 ......  ( Sb. / sth. ... so ...that... )**

- 我高興得說不出話來。I was so happy that I was speechless.
- 她看書看得連吃飯都忘了。She read so attentively that she even forgot to eat.

**Complete:**

- 我們第一次見面的時候，他_____

**Translate:**

- He was so excited that he couldn't get to sleep.

**4.** 再過 time expression ,就 **V. ...了  (Sb./sth. will [...] in + [time])**

- 再過幾天就是我妹妹的生日了。  It will be my younger sister's birthday in a few days.
- 再過一個星期,他們就要到北京去留學了。
- 再過兩個月,他就要移民到美國去了。

**Complete:**

- 再過半年,我就 _____

**Translate:**

- The movie will start in five minutes.


**5.** 爲了...... ,...... **( in order to; for the sake of)**

- 爲了把中文說好,大爲要到北京去學習。

    David will go to Beijing to study in order to speak Chinese well.
- 爲了你,我今天穿得特別漂亮。  I got all dressed up today for your sake.

**Complete:**

- 爲了我,我父母_____

**Translate:**

- In order to finish packing my luggage, I didn't sleep last night.


**6.** 對......來說,...... **( As far as Sb. is concerned...; For Sb. ... )**

- 這一次分別,對他們兩個人來說都有一點兒不容易。

    It is not easy at all for two of them to part this time.
- 他在中國住了很多年,所以對他來說,說中文一點也不難。

**Complete:**

- 對學中文的人來說,_____
- 甲 : 我很喜歡這兒的生活,你呢?

    乙 : _____

**Translate:**

- As far as I am concerned, Chinese food is the best.

For most Chinese, leaving home to go to a far-off place, especially abroad, is a serious matter. Going away not only involves the individual but concerns the entire family - grandparents, parents, brothers and sisters. Naturally it is the immediate family that is most directly concerned about the success of the traveler and the benefits that the traveler and they might receive from the trip, however other relatives and friends as well will take an active interest in the event and may even offer advice.

There are certain cultural protocols often used on these occasions. First of all, the traveler will want to visit family members and close relatives to say good-bye and seek their advice (in Chinese, 請教, qǐngjiào). In addition, visits to superiors at work to tell them of the event and seek advice is also a must-do. In Chinese this is referred to as cíxíng 辭行, 'saying goodbye.' Relatives and close friends would say their formal goodbyes and offer good wishes at a dinner party. In modern Chinese, this is called sòngbié huì 送別會.

出遠門

When the day to leave finally comes, family, relatives and friends will gather at the station or airport for a send-off, sòngxíng 送行. This custom naturally involves exchange of some 客氣話 or polite language used to show mutual concern and good wishes. The traveler might say:

我要到...去了，你有甚麼需要我幫忙
　　的嗎？

And in response, one of her relatives would most likely have said one or more of the following:

到了以後別忘了給我來信（來
　　電話，來電報）。
祝你一路順風！
祝你一路平安！
替我向你的伯母問好。

A Chinese planning to travel abroad will often hear the following kinds of remarks which are intended to reassure the person going away that everything will be handled properly in his/her absence.

你放心吧，這裡的事有我呢。
你要走了，這裡有沒有甚麼事
　　需要我幫忙？

Meeting someone coming back from far away, like the occasion of leaving, has its own customs for Chinese. Protocols may include a welcome at the station or airport. Elaborate dinners are usually given by relatives and friends in honor of the person's safe arrival after a long trip. The purpose is to demonstrate the happiness of the family after the person's safe return. The traveler, more often than not, must accept all such invitations. Declining would be an insult to the host. At the dinner party, the traveler usually brings gifts brought back from abroad chosen with special care.

# 第一課聽力練習

## 第一部分：單句

請你們聽下面的句子。每個句子的意思是什麼？請在三個選擇中選出一句來。
Listen to the recorded statements.  Circle the sentence from the three choices which is closest in meaning to the statement heard.

1. (a)小張半年前比現在胖。
   (b)小張現在只有二十公斤。
   (c)小張現在比半年前胖二十公斤。

2. (a)他一個星期送我一本書。
   (b)我最近沒看別的書，只看他送我的那本。
   (c)這一個星期裡我看了很多不同的書。

3. (a)他坐車坐得很累，所以不想做什麼事。
   (b)他累得不想坐車，也不想做事。
   (c)他做了一天事，所以現在很累。

4. (a)客人是半個鐘頭以前來的。
   (b)客人已經來了半個鐘頭了。
   (c)客人半個鐘頭以後就會來。

5. (a)他們的孩子已經到美國去留學了。
   (b)他們覺得移民到美國去對孩子好。
   (c)他們不放心把孩子送到美國去。

6. (a)喜歡電影的人大概會覺得紐約是個好地方。
   (b)紐約人都很愛看電影。
   (c)大家都覺得紐約是個好地方。

7. (a)他沒去上課是因為忘了看報。
   (b)他忘了在上課以前看報。
   (c)他看報看得太專心了，所以忘了去上課。

## 第二部分：短文

第一遍:請你們聽懂這篇短文的大意，然後回答問題。

First Listening:  Listen to the recorded story about Xiao Wang and Xiao Li.  Try to get a general idea of what it is about.  After you listen, answer the question below.

問題：小王和小李這幾個禮拜來都在忙什麼？
a)準備考試　　b)念書、看電影　　c)作出國準備

第二遍:請你們讀下面的句子，然後把這篇短文一段一段地再聽一次。聽完每一段後，看看這些句子說得對不對。

Second Listening:  Read the following statements.  Then listen to the story paragraph by paragraph and pay attention to details.  After you listen to each paragraph, decide whether the statements about it are true or false (T/F).

第一段：　____　1.小王在上大學以前就認識小李了。

　　　　　____　2.小王和小李雖然上一樣的學校，但是他們很少在一起念書。

　　　　　____　3.小王和小李都要移民到美國去了。

第二段：　____　1.小王要到美國東部去學習英國文學。

　　　　　____　2.小王和小李要到同一所學校去留學。

　　　　　____　3.小李想先把英語學好然後再念新聞。

　　　　　____　4.這一個多月來，小王和小李都在忙着和朋友告別。

I.填入適當的詞語 (Fill in the blanks with appropriate words):

1.留學：他從日本到美國來念書，他是日本＿＿＿＿＿＿＿＿＿。/他在英國留
　　了＿＿＿＿＿＿學了，英文還是說得不好。小李沒在美國留＿＿＿＿學，
　　但是英文說得真不錯。

2.準備：準備＿＿＿＿＿＿＿＿＿；準備了＿＿＿＿＿＿＿；老張就要出國了，
　　行李還沒＿＿＿＿＿＿好。出國以前應該＿＿＿＿甚麼準備？

3.分別(V.)：我是十年前＿＿＿＿＿他分別的。我們分別＿＿＿很久。/去年我
　　們分別＿＿＿兩次。 (Adv.)：我昨天分別給＿＿＿＿＿＿＿＿＿＿＿＿寫了
　　信。/他們昨天都分別來＿＿＿＿我告別。

4.移民：小王已經移民＿＿＿＿＿＿＿＿＿＿＿＿＿了。/美國有很多
　　＿＿＿＿＿＿＿＿＿來的移民。

5.約好：我們約好＿＿＿＿＿＿＿＿＿＿＿＿＿。/我＿＿＿＿＿他已經
　　＿＿＿＿＿＿＿，他一定會來。

6.見面：你跟他見＿＿＿面嗎？/我＿＿＿他見＿＿＿兩次＿＿＿。
　　我不認識他，我們從來＿＿＿＿＿＿＿＿＿。/他不住在這裡，我們很
　　少＿＿＿＿＿＿。

II.用 "會" 、 "要" 、 "想" 填空 (Fill in the blanks with 會,要 or 想):

1.　　A:你說今天＿＿＿不＿＿＿下雨？
　　　B:天氣這麼好，我想也許不＿＿＿下雨。

2.　　A:老李，聽說你＿＿＿出國了，是嗎？
　　　B:是。我明天＿＿＿去買機票。要是買到機票，下個星期就＿＿＿走。
　　　A:是嗎？走以前，別忘了告訴我，我＿＿＿請你幫我買一點兒東西。
　　　B:沒問題，我一定＿＿＿告訴你。

3.  A:小王，今天晚上你來的時候，我可能＿＿＿不在家。因爲我現在＿＿去看一個朋友，不知道什麼時候＿＿＿回來。
    B:沒關係，我來以前＿＿＿先給你打一個電話。

4.  A:我告訴你的那件事，你一定不能告訴別人。
    B:放心，我不＿＿＿告訴別人的。

III.用重疊式完成句子 (Complete the sentences using the appropriate reduplicated forms).
*Note: attach* 地 *when an actional verb follows;* 的 *is usually added when the reduplicated phrase is at the end of the clause.*

1.  他們吃了飯以後就＿＿＿＿＿＿＿＿＿＿＿＿＿＿一起出去了。(高興)
2.  她的男朋友我見過，＿＿＿＿＿＿＿＿＿，臉＿＿＿＿＿＿＿＿。（高，黑）
3.  這個人怎麼有點＿＿＿＿＿＿＿＿＿＿＿，說話的時候不看人。（怪）
4.  我把他的頭畫得＿＿＿＿＿＿＿＿，眼睛畫得＿＿＿＿＿＿＿＿。（大）
5.  時間還早呢，你＿＿＿＿＿＿＿＿＿＿＿＿＿寫吧。（慢）
6.  她來的那天穿得＿＿＿＿＿＿＿＿＿＿＿＿＿＿＿。（漂亮）
7.  我回來的時候你得把房間收拾得＿＿＿＿＿＿＿＿＿＿＿＿。（乾淨）

IV.用所給句型重寫句子 (Rewrite the sentences using the sentence patterns provided):

1.從上個星期開始到現在，我每天都在做出國準備。（這......以來，都在......）


2.飛機一個小時以後就要起飛了。（再過.....就......）


3.我這幾天太忙了，連吃飯的時間都沒有。（Adj.得......）


4.因爲我太想她了，所以常常睡不着覺。（V得......）


5.我得先學中文，這樣以後才能去中國工作。（爲了.....，......）

# 閱讀練習

Read the passage within five minutes. Look up unfamiliar words in your dictionary or figure out meanings from the context. After reading, answer the questions.

　　小張以前是北京一個大學的學生，在大學的時候他的學習很好。畢業以後他一直很想到美國去留學，所以就寫信給一個美國的親戚請他幫忙申請一個學校。上個星期他收到了親戚的回信，裡面還有一封學校的信，信上說他可以到美國去留學了。小張看了這封信以後興奮得不得了，他的親戚朋友也都很高興。這幾天來，他都在做出國準備：申請護照和簽證、買機票、收拾行李，還要跟親友們告別，所以忙得團團轉。

　　雖然小張的親戚朋友都很高興，可是小張的女朋友却<u>悶悶不樂</u>。她跟小張是半年以前在<u>辦公室</u>裡認識的，這半年以來他們天天都在一起工作，星期天也一起出去玩，很快樂。可是現在小張要走了，而且不知道什麼時候才會回來，她心裡很不舒服。這幾天小張因爲忙着出國的事，連跟她在一起說話的時間都沒有了。她想如果小張到美國去了以後，一定很快就會把她忘了的。所以她這幾天吃不下飯，睡不着覺。她想她得跟小張好好談談。

<u>下面說的對不對？如果不對，是哪裡不對？請寫出來</u>。

1. 小張以前是北京大學的學生。

2. 小張現在已經工作了。

3. 小張是自己跟美國的學校申請留學的。

4. 小張忙得團團轉，所以沒有時間跟親戚朋友告別了。

5. 小張跟他的女朋友是在大學裡認識的。

6. 小張的女朋友覺得小張去美國不好，因爲她不能跟小張在一起了。

7. 小張的女朋友這幾天睡不着覺，因爲小張沒有時間跟她說話。

8. "悶悶不樂" (mènmèn bú lè) 的意思是不太高興。

# 口語練習

I.<u>解釋生詞</u> (Explain the following words in Chinese within your vocabulary range. One example is given):

（例）： <u>移民</u>：移民就是從一個國家到另一個國家去住的人。
收拾行李；護照；簽證；分別；親戚

II.<u>小對話</u> (Mini-talks): Make short conversations with the topics provided. Try to focus on these elements: when, who, where, for what, how, for how long. Two examples are provided.

話題:回國看親戚；跟新老師見面；申請留學；做出國準備；收拾行李

<u>例1 (Example 1)</u>:要做的事情
A:小李,我要到中國去留學了。B:真的？<u>什麼時候走</u>？要去多久？
A:<u>下個月</u>就走了,要去一年。　B:你<u>一個人去</u>還是跟<u>別人一起去</u>？
A:我跟我的同學一起去。　　B:那一定很有意思！你們準備<u>從哪兒</u>走？
A:我想<u>從紐約</u> (Niǔyuē)走。　B:祝你一路順風！

<u>例2(Example 2)</u>:已經做了的事情
A:小張,你到哪兒去了？好久不見！B:噢(Ao),我到中國留學去了。
A:真的？你<u>什麼時候去的</u>？　　B:去年八月。
A:<u>去了多久</u>？　　　　　　B:差不多一年。我上星期剛回來。
A:你<u>學得怎麼樣</u>？　　　　B:很累。不過,我也玩得很開心。
A:你以前<u>留過學</u>嗎？　　　B:沒有。這是第一次。

III.<u>情景會話</u> (Situational Conversation)

<u>練習1:談為什麼要出國留學</u>
　　假設你想出國留學,可是你的父母覺得你不應該現在出國。你要想辦法說服他們。（請和兩個同學一起,練習你和父母的談話。）

<u>練習2:談自己的情況</u>
　　假設你現在在中國學習。第一次上課的時候,老師想知道你是從哪個國家來的,你是在哪裡長大的,你為什麼到中國來學中文。請你告訴老師同學你的情況。

# 寫作練習

練習 1.談出國

　　如果你出過國，請說一說你去過什麼地方。你出國以前做了一些什麼準備？是怎麼去的？跟誰一起去的？為什麼去？去以前你想那個地方會是什麼樣？到了以後你看見的是不是跟你想的一樣？有什麼有意思的事情？你在那裡待了多久？你玩得高興嗎？還想再去一次嗎？

有用的詞彙 (Useful Vocabulary/Expressions):

敍述 (for narration):

| | | | |
|---|---|---|---|
| 會/要/想 | 當時 | 以前/以後 | 後來 |
| 得+complement | 再過……就 | 這……以來 | 是……的 |

比較 (for comparing):

A跟B（不）一樣；　　A比B……；　　　A沒有B（那麼）…；

有的…,有的…；　　雖然…可是…；　　因為…所以…；不但…而且…

練習 2.看圖習作 (Tell a story based on the pictures)

## "小王第一次出國"

# "你就是李大爲同學吧？"

## —到達北京—

## 第二課

| Situation | Structure | Culture |
|-----------|-----------|---------|
| 語言情景 | 語言結構 | 文化介紹 |

In Lesson Two, David (李大爲), after a long trip, finally arrives in Beijing, meets his teachers and makes some new friends.

You'll concentrate on creating focus with two types of "presentative sentences."

You'll learn about custom and language when you introduce yourself (介紹自己) and introduce others (介紹別人).

# "你就是李大爲同學吧？"
## --到達北京--

大爲的飛機總算到了北京。下了飛機、拿到行李以後，他就趕快出了機場。機場出口處有很多人，有的手裡拿着寫着人名的牌子[i]，有的向走出機場的人大聲叫。大爲看來看去，就是找不到一個寫着"李大爲"三個字的牌子。他想，怪了！收到的信上明明寫着有人會在機場出口處等他，可是人在哪兒呢？會不會是他們記錯了飛機到達的時間？還是自己回信的時候把到達的日期寫錯了？看樣子得自己找到學校去了。可是他也不清楚學

校到底在哪兒、離這兒到底有多遠。只好坐出租車吧，司機總[ii]會知道這個學校在哪兒的。

大爲正要叫出租車，突然看見前面走過來幾個人[iii]，其中有一個人手裡拿着一個牌子，上面寫着"北京大學漢語中心"幾個字。大爲一看高興極了，趕快走過去。

---

i. Note this sentence-type where a Place Word (手裡) + Verb着 (拿着) + something (人名的牌子), inverts the usual Chinese word order. We call this the Presentative Sentence. See **Focusing on Structure**, in this lesson, for a detailed explanation and examples.

ii. 總 is a tonal adverb used in speech with many usages. Some common meanings (not illustrated in the text) include "anyway", "cannot but", "at least", "sooner or later", etc.

iii. 前面走過來幾個人 is another example of the Presentative Sentence (inverted word order). See Note i above.

| | | | |
|---|---|---|---|
| 同學 | 同学 | tóngxué | N classmate, fellow student (同 , "same" prefixed to nouns) |
| 到達 | 到达 | dàodá | V/N to reach, arrive; arrival |
| 總算 | 总算 | zǒngsuàn | MA at long last, finally (for 總 see Note ii) |
| 趕快 | 赶快 | gǎnkuài | A hurriedly, quickly |
| 出口處 | 出口处 | chūkǒuchù | N exit (出口 N exit; -處 -place, Noun-Suffix) |
| 牌子 | | páizi | N sign; brand (of a product) |
| 向 | | xiàng | CV toward, to |
| 明明 | | míngmíng | A clearly, obviously |
| 日期 | | rìqī | N date |
| 到底 | | dàodǐ | MA after all |
| 離 | 离 | lí | CV (distance) from (in space/time) |
| 遠 | 远 | yuǎn | ADJ far |
| 出租 | | chūzū | V lease out; leased. |
| 　出租車 | 出租车 | chūzūchē | N taxi ('Taxi' is 計程車 [jìchéngchē] in Taiwan) |
| 司機 | 司机 | sījī | N chauffeur, driver |
| 突然 | | tūrán | MA/ADJ suddenly, abruptly; abrupt |
| 其中 | | qízhōng | PW among them; in which |
| 面 | | miàn | N side |
| 　上面 | | shàngmiàn | PW on top of, on, above (syn. 上頭,上邊 ); |
| 中心 | | zhōngxīn | N center |

大爲：你們好！你們是不是來接我的？我
　　　的名字叫李大爲，David Leigh，從美
　　　國來的。

張：噢（Ò），你就是李大爲同學啊？好
　　極了！我們正等你呢。歡迎你到北
　　京來！

林：李大爲同學，歡迎歡迎！我來<sup>iv</sup>給你
　　介紹一下：這位是張老師，是我們
　　學校留學生辦公室的。我叫林紅，
　　是中文班的老師。

大爲：張老師，林老師，謝謝你們來接我！

林：不客氣，這是我們應該做的。這位是剛到的法國留學生，叫——亞
　　可，對不對？

雅克：不是亞可，是雅克。雅是高雅的雅，克是克制的克。

大爲：認識你很高興，雅克。

雅克：我也很高興認識你。

張：大爲同學，坐這麼長時間的飛機，辛苦了吧？

大爲：還<sup>v</sup>可以。我真不敢相信我現在已經在北京了！

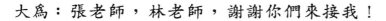

iv. 來 presents several usages in this lesson, in addition to its meaning of "come."
　　a. As a kind of `helping/dummy verb' which preceeds an action verb in an imperative sentence.
　　我來給你們介紹一下。　Let me introduce you to each other.
　　這件事你來做，怎麼樣？ (I'll let) You do this job. How is that?
　　b. Stands in for an understood verb in imperative sentences.
　　你不必幫我拿行李，我自己來。（來 stands in for 來拿）No need to help with the luggage; I'll
　　　do it myself.
　　誰唸一下這個句？小王，你來。（來 for 來唸: Who will read this? Xiao Wang, you do it.)
　　c. As an 'initiator' to suggest an action. ("Now" "Come on")
　　來，我幫你拿行李。　Come on, let me (I'll) help you with your luggage.
　　來，我們快上車吧。　Come on, let's get on the bus (van, train, car, etc.)

v. 還 is often used to convey the sense "sort of", "moderately" or "fairly", as in 還好 (pretty good), 還可以
　　(OK),還不錯 (quite good). 還 in these usages does not occur with such negative words as 壞 (bad),不好
　　(not good), 難 (difficult), and others, all of which have negative connotations.

林：你是第一次來北京嗎？

大為：是，可是夢裡已經來過好幾次了。

雅克：我也是，可是我夢裡的北京機場好像跟這裡不一樣。

張：那不奇怪。要是一樣了就真奇怪了。我希望你們看到的北京比夢裡
　　的更好。來<sup>vi</sup>，快上車吧。小林，幫大為同學拿一下行李。

大為：不用不用，我自己來<sup>vii</sup>。

林：別客氣了，走吧。


| 接 | | jiē | V to pick up/meet (sb. at a station, airport, etc.); to receive (mail, phone call, etc.) |
|---|---|---|---|
| 歡迎 | 欢迎 | huānyíng | V/N to welcome; welcome |
| 辦公室 | 办公室 | bàngōngshì | N office, workplace (辦公, VO to work [in an office]); (-室, -room) |
| 林紅 | 林红 | Lín Hóng | N (name of a person) |
| 亞可 | 亚可 | Yàkě | N (one common transliteration for 'Jacques') |
| 雅克 | | Yǎkè | N (another common transliteration for 'Jacques') |
| 高雅 | | gāoyǎ | ADJ elegant |
| 克制 | | kèzhì | V/N restrain, suppress; restraint, suppression |
| 辛苦 | | xīnkǔ | ADJ/N laborious, toilsome; toil |
| 還可以 | 还可以 | hái kěyǐ | IE so-so, passable |
| 敢 | | gǎn | AV to dare to |
| 相信 | | xiāngxìn | V to believe |

---

vi & vii. See Note iv (examples b and c).

判斷出以下詞語的意思：

機場出口處　　　机场出口处
大聲　　　　　　大声
回信
留學生　　　　　留学生

回答下面的問題：

1.大為下了飛機以後為什麼要趕快出機場？
2.在出口處接人的人多不多？他們怎麼找他們要接的人？
3.大為沒看見來接他的人的時候怎麼想？
4.為什麼大為沒有叫出租車？
5.來接大為的是什麼人？
6.雅克也是來接大為的嗎？

# 語言結構
## Focusing on Structure

**Presentative Sentences With Inverted Word Order: Sentence-end as Focus**

Presentative sentences refer to sentences in which a normally pre-verbal element (e.g. the performer of an action) is moved to the post-verbal position. Such inversion is not uncommon in English or other languages, as shown by "In the room stood a man", "Here comes the train" or "Once upon a time there lived a man named...." Through such inversion, the noun being introduced into the discourse (but now at the end of the clause) becomes the focus. In Chinese, two types of these presentative inversions are commonly used:

**I. Durative/on-going State: Location + Verb-着 + Noun:**

Verbs used in this type are typically those that denote physical disposition (posture verbs), for example 站, 坐, or 睡, or location-oriented action verbs, such as 住, 貼, 寫, or 放. These verbs occur with the durative marker -着, to signal the ongoing nature of a state or an action.

門口站着一個小男孩。

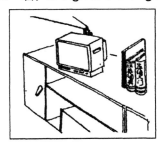

桌上放着一個電視機和幾本書。

牆上掛着一個牌子，
上面畫着一隻狗。

**II. Action/Event:  Location/Time + Action Verb + indefinite Actor:**

Verbs used in this type are always intransitive (verbs which do not take objects) denoting appearance or disappearance (e.g. 來, 出來, 走了)    or actions involving movement/locomotion with verbs of 來 or 走 (e.g. 走過來, 跑出來, 搬走).
Some examples:

突然，房子裡跑出來一隻狗。

雨下得很大，這時，前面開來一輛車。

**CAUTION:**

a. Type I sentences do not use verbs such as 吃，考試，看書，做事 which are not location oriented.

Type I:　　飯館裡 <u>吃着</u>一個人。（ Wrong because verb is not location-oriented)
　　　　　　桌上<u>站着</u>一個電視機。(Wrong verb used; should be 放 )

b. Type II sentences do not use transitive verbs or verbs that do not denote appearance/disappearance or locomotion, such as 看書，做事，買東西，笑，喜歡，懂，看見.

Type II:　　大樓那裡 <u>看見</u>兩個人。(Wrong because verb used is transitive and not appearance or locomotional)
　　　　　　房子裡面<u>出</u>一個人。(出來 or 走出來 should be used.)

# 辭彙用法
## Word Usage

### Verbs
- 找：找人；找房子；找工作；找了半天；找得很辛苦；找到了一個工作；找不到工作
- 到達：到達紐約；到達的時間；到達的日期；你的飛機幾點到達北京？
- 介紹：介紹一個朋友；介紹一個工作；把她介紹給小王；我來給你們介紹一下。
- 接：接電話；接一個人；到機場去接朋友
- 希望：我希望你明天早一點來。/希望不大(N)
- 相信：我不相信他的話。/我相信你會學好中文。

### Verb-Object Compounds
- 回信：給他回信；回了幾封信；我現在沒時間給他回信。

### Resultative Verb Compounds
- 記錯：記錯時間；記錯日期；記錯地點；把考試的日期記錯了；沒記錯
- 接到：昨天去機場接他，等了三個鐘頭才接到。/這幾天接不到他的電話。

### Auxiliary Verbs
- 敢：你敢不敢做這件事？/你長這麼大了——我真不敢相信我的眼睛！

### Adjectives/Adverbs
- 辛苦：辛辛苦苦地工作；他的生活很辛苦。/學中文一點也不辛苦。
- 遠：很遠的地方；我家離學校不遠。/他已經走遠了。
- 客氣：客客氣氣；別客氣；不必跟我客氣。/對人很客氣；他說話不太客氣。
- 總算：我總算把行李收拾好了。/你總算聽懂我的話了。
- 趕快：天黑了，我們還是趕快回家吧。/大家都在等你，你趕快來吧。
- 到底：學校到底在哪裡？/這個人到底是誰？/飛機到底是幾點到達？/你到底去不去？
- 突然：上課的時候他突然笑了起來，大家都覺得很奇怪。/這件事很突然。
- 好像：我好像在哪兒見過他。/他好像不是中國人。/你今天好像很累的樣子。

### Coverbs
- 向：向東走；向左走；向前走；向後看；向他大聲叫；他向我們走過來。
- 離：這兒離學校有多遠？/我家離飛機場不遠。/現在離上課還有五分鐘。

### Nouns
- 牌子：拿着一個牌子；門上有一個牌子。/這個牌子(brand)很有名。
- 夢：做夢；做了好幾個夢；昨天晚上我夢見（夢到）一個老朋友。

## I. Presentative Sentences:

**1. Location +V 着+ sb./ sth. (There at [place] [verb] sth./sb.)**

* 門上貼着一張字條。

  On the door is/was attached a note./ A note is/was attached to the door.
* 教室裡坐着幾個學生。
* 桌子上放着一個杯子，幾本中文書，和一張飛機票。

**Complete:**

* 甲：你手裡拿着什麼？

  乙：我 _____

**Translate:**

* On that sheet of paper there are written the three characters, "我走了."

**2. Location/Time + [appearance/disappearance] Verb + Noun (doer, etc.)**

* 我看見前面走過來幾個人。 I saw a few people walk up from the distance.
* 教室裡突然跑進（來）一隻狗。 A dog suddenly ran into the classroom.
* 昨天我家裡來了一些人。

**Translate:**

* A lot of people left (走了) a moment ago.

## II. Additional Useful Sentence Patterns

**1. V來V去，就是 (neg.)... ( Sb. kept doing sth. but just couldn't / didn't... )**

* 我想來想去，就是想不出一個好法子來。

  I thought about it over and over, but I just couldn't come up with a good idea.
* 他找來找去，就是找不到他的護照。

**Complete:**

* 甲：你的中文學得怎麼樣了？
* 乙：我 _____

**Translate:**

- I kept writing these characters, but I just couldn't write them well.

**2. 看樣子......(It seems/looks like... )**

- 看樣子他不會來了。 It seems he is not coming.
- 看樣子這件事不是他的錯。 It seems to me that this is not his fault.

**Complete:**

- 他連這麼簡單的字都不會寫，看樣子＿＿＿＿＿＿＿＿＿＿＿＿＿＿

**Translate：**

- It looks like you don't believe what I've said.

**3. .....，其中......( ......, among whom/which; of which ... )**

- 我有二十本書，其中有五本中文書。
  I have twenty books, five of which are Chinese books.
- 這個班有三十個學生，其中一半是美國人。

**Translate:**

- She has been to many places, among which she likes New York most.

**4. Sb.是第一次......( It is sb's first time...... )**

- 你是第一次來美國嗎？ Is this your first time in America?
- 我是第一次用筷子吃飯，所以覺得有一點不習慣。

**Complete:**

- 甲：你以前學過中文嗎？乙：沒有，＿＿＿＿＿＿＿＿＿＿＿＿＿

**Translate:**

- Is this their first time on an airplane?

Learning About Culture
介紹別人與自我介紹
**Introducing Others and Introducing Oneself**

When Americans introduce people to one another, they often make distinctions reflecting, for example, the status of the people involved. For example, if you were to introduce your friend, Mary, to your grandmother, you might say: "Grandma, this is my friend Mary," followed by, "Mary, this is my grandma, Mrs. Smith." Chinese take this attention to status a step further when making introductions, taking into account both age and social position. When making introductions, Chinese will normally first state the surname of the person to be introduced, then his/her title, and sometimes mention briefly what the person does for a living and even sometimes their accomplishments. As a foreigner, you have to keep in mind the requirement that some sort of title be included when making introductions, either a job title or a social title, like Mr. or Mrs., etc.

Here are some examples of professional titles: Lǐ xiàozhǎng (李校長: Principal Lǐ), Wáng yīshēng (王醫生: Dr. Wáng), Bái zhǔrèn (白主任: Director Bái), or Zhāng lǎoshī (張老師: Teacher Zhāng). Job or professional titles will take precedence over social titles.

The 'social' titles used mainly include the ones already familiar to you, like, Fàn Xiānsheng (范先生: Mr. Fàn),

Gāo Tàitai (高太太: Mrs. Gāo), Wáng Xiǎojiě or Wáng Yīrú Xiǎojiě (王小姐/王一如小姐: Miss Wáng or Miss Wáng Yīrú).

What about given names? Well, given names can be included but must follow the surname. Just giving the given name without the surname is avoided as overly familiar or intimate, especially if the given name is monosyllabic.

In less formal situations, the full name alone can be used in an introduction. For example, Zhāng Yīlín (張一林), Lǐ Mànyún (李曼云). But in no circumstances will only the surname be used, such as "Zhāng" (張).

When introducing themselves, Chinese use their full name, without any title (to avoid showiness). It is also inappropriate to introduce oneself as a specialist of such and such, like "an anthropologist," "a scientist," "a historian," and the like. If one wishes to identify what one does, one can say, for example, "I am a person who studies history." (我是學歷史的 or 我是搞文學的。 (I do literature./I'm in literature.)

When Chinese give their names orally (either simply the surname or the whole name), it is common for the person to identify the Chinese characters of the surname or given name by associating the characters with a commonly-used word composed of the same characters or by describing the structure of the surname/given name-characters. For example, if named "李方", one might say " 木子李的李 " (The Lǐ composed of 木 and 子), " 地方的方 " (the fāng of 地方 ). This method of identification is necessary due to the large number of characters that have the same pronunciation.

Finally, Chinese people often use conventional phrases such as jiǔyǎng! jiǔyǎng! (久仰久仰 "I've [long] heard wonderful things about you.") to a well-known person; or xìnghuì! xìnghuì! (幸會幸會 "I'm so fortunate to meet you!") as a polite response after being introduced.

Here are some examples of words and phrases commonly used in introductions:

- 你就是劉新民先生吧？我是白文山。
- 我來（給你們）介紹一下：這是張海新教授，教歷史的，這是白文山老師，搞文學的。
- 來，認識一下，這是我的同屋，愛德華。
- 請問貴姓？
- 請問大名？
- 我姓李，叫李大爲：木子李，大小的大，作爲的爲。
- 您好。很高興認識您。/很高興（今天在這兒）見到您。
- 請問你是哪裡（哪國）人？
- 馬老師常常說起您。/常常听人說起您（的名字）。
- 久仰！久仰！(jiǔyǎng)
- 幸會！幸會！(xìnghuì)

# 第二課聽力練習

## 第一部分：單句

請你們聽下面的句子。每個句子的意思是什麼？請在三個選擇中選出一句來。
Listen to the recorded statements. Circle the sentence from the three choices which is closest in meaning to the statement heard.

1. (a)有一個台灣留學生想住進這個房子裡。
   (b)有一個台灣留學生住在這個房子裡。
   (c)這個房子裡只有一個人住着。

2. (a)很多像留學生的人從機場裡走了出來。
   (b)很多留學生在機場裡走來走去。
   (c)從機場裡走出來的都是留學生。

3. (a)人們都喜歡在上午申請工作。
   (b)這兒的人上午都不工作。
   (c)今天上午有很多人來這兒申請工作。

4. (a)車上的外國人中文都說得很好。
   (b)有兩個說着中文的外國人從車上下來了。
   (c)很多外國人下了車，其中有兩個是男的。

5. (a)我看了又看，可是還是不知道這本書爲什麼好。
   (b)這本書我看了半天才看懂。
   (c)這本書寫得很好，所以我看了很多次。

6. (a)小王的父母第一次出國的時候很興奮。
   (b)小王的父母要出國了，他覺得很不放心。
   (c)小王的父母很不放心，因爲小王以前沒出過國。

第一遍:請你們聽懂這篇短文的大意，然後回答問題。
First Listening:  Listen to the recorded story.  Try to get a general idea of what it is about. After you listen, answer the question.

問題：小王剛找到一個什麼工作？

　　　　　a)教中文的工作　　　　　b)教英文的工作

第二遍:請你們讀下面的句子，然後把這篇短文一段一段地再聽一次。聽
　　　完每一段後，看看這些句子說得對不對。
Second Listening:  Read the following statements.  Then listen to the story paragraph by paragraph and pay attention to details.  After you listen to each paragraph, decide whether the statements about it are true or false.

第一段：　　____　　1.小王現在在一個大學裡教中文。

　　　　　　____　　2.小王今天一大早就到教室去等學生。

　　　　　　____　　3.小王在林老師辦公室的門口看見了幾個外國人。

　　　　　　____　　4.從林老師辦公室走出來的那幾個人看見小王時都向他
　　　　　　　　　　問好。

第二段：　　____　　1.穿紅衣服的女孩在小王的中文班上。

　　　　　　____　　2.小王一到教室就開始上課。

　　　　　　____　　3.穿紅衣服的女孩是在美國東部長大的。

　　　　　　____　　4.穿紅衣服的女孩以前來過台灣。

　　　　　　____　　5.穿紅衣服的女孩要在台灣學兩個月的中文。

# 第二課 練習
## 辭彙；句型；語法

I.選擇適當的詞語 (Circle the most appropriate word from those provided in the parentheses):

1.飛機已經飛了兩天了，為甚麼還沒＿＿＿＿＿＿紐約？（來，到達）

2.我的護照我找了兩天，＿＿＿＿＿＿＿找到了。（總會，總算）

3.申請表上為什麼沒有寫出國的＿＿＿＿＿＿？（時候，日期）

4.下午我們就要上飛機了，你＿＿＿＿＿收拾行李吧！（很快地，趕快）

5.昨天我們上課的時候＿＿＿＿＿＿進來一個人。（當然，突然）

6.小李昨天晚上請客，＿＿＿＿＿＿大為到北京來。（歡迎，接）

7.我把小李＿＿＿＿＿＿給小王。（認識，介紹，見面）

II.翻譯"來"字的意思或用法 (Translate the meaning/usage of 來 in each sentence):

1.我來給你們兩個介紹一下。這位是......　＿＿＿＿＿＿＿＿＿

2.我去叫出租車，誰替我看一下行李？——我來吧。＿＿＿＿＿＿＿＿

3.來，我幫你收拾房間。——不用不用，我自己來。＿＿＿＿＿＿＿＿

4.來，我們快上飛機吧。＿＿＿＿＿＿＿＿

5.昨天來了兩個美國留學生。＿＿＿＿＿＿＿＿＿＿＿＿

III.改寫句子 (Rewrite the following sentences applying the patterns provided):

1.這麼晚了，他好像不會來了。（看樣子......）


2.這個字我寫了好多次了，可是還是寫不好。（V來V去,就是.....）


3.我看見桌子上有幾本書，牆上有一張畫。（V着）


4.你以前出過國嗎？（......第一次......）


5.這個班二十多個學生裡有五個中國人。（.....,其中有....）

IV. 填空 (Fill in the blanks with appropriate words):

1. 存現倒裝句 (Presentative sentences with inverted word order: Location V着 ...)

我走進一間屋子，看見牀上＿＿＿＿着一個小男孩，好像睡着了。他頭上＿＿＿＿着一個紅帽子，手裡 ＿＿＿＿着一個小飛機。桌子上有一張條子，上面＿＿＿＿着一些英文。桌子那兒還＿＿＿着兩把椅子。我正要走出屋子的時候，門外突然＿＿＿＿＿＿來一隻大狗，然後又＿＿＿＿＿＿＿＿來兩個人。

2. 語氣副詞 (Tonal adverbs: choose from 還、總、真、才、總算)

a) 我在那裡住了兩天，那兒的天氣＿＿＿不錯！　　　　（才；真；總）

b) 他說我很怪，我覺得他＿＿＿＿真的怪呢。　　　　　（才；還；總算）

c) 他的中文說得＿＿＿＿＿可以，可是寫得不好。　　　（真；總；還）

d) 你＿＿＿＿＿傻！怎麼能把錢給一個不認識的人？　　（總算；還；真）

e) 他現在不知道這件事，以後 ＿＿＿＿＿＿會知道的。　（總；總算；才）

f) 你跟他是好朋友，你要走了，＿＿＿得跟他告別一下吧？（真；才；總）

g) 我高興得不得了，今天＿＿＿＿＿考完試了！　　　　（真；總算；總）

3. 用適當的 "動詞—到" 形式 (Use appropriate V到 form)

a) 他到那邊去拿行李，可是人太多，他等了十分鐘還＿＿＿＿＿＿。

b) 我昨天去機場接一個朋友，等了三個鐘頭才＿＿＿＿＿＿。

c) 我找來找去，就是＿＿＿＿＿＿你的護照。

d) 昨天晚上我做了一個夢，你猜我＿＿＿＿＿＿誰了？

V. 用 "到底" 加強語氣 (Intensify your tone by using 到底)

a) 你去不去？　　　　　　　　　　　　　＿＿＿＿＿＿＿＿＿＿＿＿＿＿＿

b) 誰去？你去還是他去？　　　　　　　　＿＿＿＿＿＿＿＿＿＿＿＿＿＿＿

c) 今天去還是明天去？　　　　　　　　　＿＿＿＿＿＿＿＿＿＿＿＿＿＿＿

d) 他是在哪裡生的？　　　　　　　　　　＿＿＿＿＿＿＿＿＿＿＿＿＿＿＿

e) 這種電腦好不好？哪一個電腦好？　　　＿＿＿＿＿＿＿＿＿＿＿＿＿＿＿

f) 他是誰？他是學什麼的？　　　　　　　＿＿＿＿＿＿＿＿＿＿＿＿＿＿＿

# 閱讀練習

1. (4 minutes): Read the passage through without stopping in order to grasp the general idea. When you finish, try to collect the information you have read.
2. (6 minutes): Read the passage again. Mark the words you don't understand and pay special attention to the underlined words. You may look them up in the dictionary later.
3. Answer the True/False questions.

　　張明要回國去<u>休假</u>，在<u>機場</u>碰到了他以前的大學同學李琳。他們在大學的時候都是學英文的，三年以前一起到美國來留學。小張在美國東部的一個大學學電腦，小李在西部學<u>經濟學</u>(Economics)。他們倆從那次在舊金山(San Francisco)的機場<u>告別</u>以後就沒有<u>再見過面</u>；所以今天見到，他們都很<u>興奮</u>。小張告訴小李，他從到了美國以後，就<u>好好地</u>學了兩年電腦。去年他<u>畢業</u>了，在一家公司裡找到了一個工作。這一年來他工作得很<u>辛苦</u>，現在想要回國去玩<u>一段時間</u>。

　　小李說她也是要回國去一趟，<u>不過</u>不是她一個人回去，而是和她的男朋友一起去。她還沒念完博士(Ph.D.)，還得一兩年才念得完。她的男朋友是美國人，是她的同學，名字叫約翰(Yuēhàn: John)。約翰是學<u>東亞</u>經濟的，對中國經濟<u>特別有興趣</u>。他學過幾年中文，中文說得很<u>不錯</u>，字也寫得很漂亮。不過他還沒有去過中國，很想去看看。小李寫信回去告訴父母她找了一個會說中文的美國男朋友，還把約翰寫的字也一起<u>寄</u>回去給他們看。母親回信說，父親是一個很保守的中國人，從來沒有想到過自己的女儿會找一個美國人。不過他們都願意見見這位會說中文也會寫中國字的 "老外" ，很高興小李帶約翰到家裡去玩。這就是小李這次回國的<u>原因</u>。

<u>下面說的對不對？如果不對，是哪裡不對？怎麼才對？請寫出來。</u>

1.小張和小李已經在美國住了差不多三年了。

2.小張和小李現在是美國東部一個大學的同學。

3.小李的學習不好，所以她還沒有畢業。

4.小張在公司裡工作了兩年了。

5.小李和小張差不多一年沒有見面了。

6.約翰是在中國學的中文，所以他的中文說得很好。

7.小李回國是為了約翰，因為約翰很想去中國。

# 口語練習

I.請你用中文說出下面這些詞的意思：

　　　司機；出租車；留學生；辦公室

II.應答練習:(One student SAYS --not reads--the sentence, another student responds by making a comment, answering/asking a question, etc. according to the situation given.)

例 E.g.: A:我今天才知道小李不是北京人。

　　　　B:那他是哪裡的人呢？（ or:我早就知道了。/是他告訴你的嗎？etc.）

a)看樣子明天我會很忙，不能跟你出去玩了。

b)我找來找去，就是找不到他給我的那封信。

c)快看，前面跑過來三個人！後面還跟着 (follow)一隻大狗！

d)哎呀 (àiyā) 你總算來了！我等你等了半個鐘頭了！

e)我叫張大爲，是來接你的。

f)你坐了這麼長時間的飛機，一定很辛苦吧？

g)我很喜歡北京，我是第二次來北京了。

h)你手裡拿着的那本書明明是我的，你爲什麼不還給我？

III.情景會話:

練習一：問別人情況/談個人情況

　　　　你到了一個新的中文班，需要認識新同學。找一個同學，先介紹自己；然後問他/她：姓名、是哪裡人、在哪裡生的、哪裡長大的、在學校學什麼、喜歡什麼、爲什麼學中文。（最少認識兩個人）。請注意說自己中文名字的時候得說清楚是哪幾個字（如：木子李，聰明的明）。

練習二：介紹別人

　　　　把你剛才分別認識的人介紹給另一個。請用下面這些句子：

1.　　我來給你們介紹一下。這位是.....，他是......。這位是......,他是......。

2.　　你好。認識你很高興。/你好，我也很高興認識你。

3.　　你喜歡這個學校嗎？/你都喜歡些什麼？

IV. <u>描述和敘述練習</u>：一件事的經過 (Telling about an event)

　　看下面的圖，把事情的經過說出來。請用新學的倒裝結構
(Place V 着 ; Place V + performer).

　　地鐵：[dìtiě] subway　　　袋子：[dàizi] bag, sack　　警察：[jǐngchá] cop

　　刀：　[dāo] knife　　　　　乘客：[chéngkè] passenger　槍：[qiāng] gun

(Follow the guide below.)

　　有一天晚上我……。地鐵裡人不多，我旁邊……，前邊還……，在看報
紙。這時候，突然……一個男人，他頭上……,手裡……。他對一個女乘客說，
"……！" 那個女的說，"……" 然後趕快把……。就在這時 ….一個警察，手
裡……。他大聲叫，"……！" 壞人一看不好，趕快……。

# 寫作練習

看圖習作：(請用新學的用法：Location V-着 ...。Follow the guide below)

　　這張圖畫的是.....，可能是......。房間裡有一張牀，還有一張書桌。牀上......，他在......。桌上......，還.......，其中有一本是......。牆上......，有一張上面......"......"幾個字。地上......。看樣子這個人是一個......，他可能很喜歡......。

有用的詞彙 Useful Vocabulary

躺 [tǎng] to lie on the back　　球拍 [qiúpāi] racket　　辭典 [cídiǎn] dictionary

足球 [zúqiú] soccer　　運動 [yùndòng] exercise　　英漢辭典 English-Chinese dictionary

籃球 [lánqiú] basketball　　運動員 athlete　　收音機 [shōuyīnjī] radio

網球 [wǎngqiú] tennis　　電腦 [diànnǎo] computer　　收錄機 [shōulùjī] tape-player

# "聽我的，沒錯！"

## ─ 介紹對象 ─

第三課

| Situation | Structure | Culture |
|-----------|-----------|---------|
| 語言情景 | 語言結構 | 文化介紹 |

Here in Lesson Three you'll join Helen in Taibei as she talks with her aunt about a personal matter and is provided with some unexpected personal advice.

You'll re-visit (see Lesson One) the structures used to make language more vivid with adjective reduplication.

You'll also discover how to soften language tone with reduplicated verbs and look into some other useful language patterns and expressions.

Culturally, you'll look into Chinese notions about marriage and family.

# "聽我的，沒錯！"
## --介紹對象--

　　大爲走了兩天以後，海琳也坐飛機到了台北。 海琳這次到台北來有兩個原因：一是伯母多次寫信給她父母，説好幾年沒有看見海琳了，很想見見她。現在海琳畢業了，該到台灣來玩玩了。二是海琳主修的是東亞經濟，她想先在台灣找個工作，熟悉熟悉台灣的情況。

　　海琳住在親戚家裡，什麼都很方便，就是有一點她不太習慣：伯母太愛管她的閒事。伯母是一個很能幹的人，可是也有一點自以爲是，家裡的事不管大小都得她一個人安排和決定。她雖然一天到晚爲自己家的事忙得團團轉，可是還喜歡爲別人的事忙，尤其喜歡給人介紹對象。她知道海琳要在台灣待一段時間，所以想藉這個機會給海琳也介紹一個對象。

你這次來得正好，我要給你介紹一個對象。

"對象"是什麼？

| | | | |
|---|---|---|---|
| 對象 | 对象 | duìxiàng | N (marriage) prospect; target, object |
| 原因 | | yuányīn | N reason, cause |
| 伯母 | | bómǔ | N wife of father's elder brother; aunt |
| 畢業 | 毕业 | bìyè | VO/N to graduate; graduation |
| 台灣 | 台湾 | Táiwān | PW Taiwan |
| 主修 | | zhǔxiū | V/N to major (in); major (in college) |
| 亞 | 亚 | yà | Asia (used as suffix, but also as prefix (亞洲, Yàzhōu, Asia) |
| 東亞 | 东亚 | Dōngyà | PW East Asia |
| 經濟 | 经济 | jīngjì | ADJ/N economical; economics, economy |
| 熟悉 | | shóuxi/shúxi | V/ADJ to be/become quite familiar (with), know sth. or sb. well; acquainted with |
| 情況 | 情况 | qíngkuàng | N situation, condition, status |
| 管 | | guǎn | V to manage, take care [of a matter], in charge of |
| 管閒事 | 管闲事 | guǎn xiánshì | VP to butt into other people's business |
| 能幹 | 能干 | nénggàn | ADJ capable, able |
| 自以為是 | 自以为是 | zì yǐ wéi shì | PH to regard oneself as right; disregard the opinions of others |
| 不管 | | bùguǎn | MA no matter, regardless |
| 安排 | | ānpái | V/N to arrange, schedule; arrangement |
| 待 | | dāi | V to stay (at a place or for a time) |
| 藉 | 借 | jiè | V by means of, take (opportunity/ advantage to do sth.) |
| 機會 | 机会 | jīhuì | N chance, opportunity |

伯母：海琳啊，你這次來得正好。
　　　我要給你介紹一個對象。

海琳："對象"是什麼？

伯母：哎呀，二十多歲的人了，連
　　　"對象"是什麼都不知道啊？
　　　對象就是談戀愛的朋友，懂了
　　　吧？也就是——以後跟你結婚
　　　的人。

海琳：什麼？結婚？！我還小[i]呢，
　　　我可[ii]不想結婚。

伯母：咳(Hai)！誰要你現在結婚了？可是以後你總得結婚吧？結婚總得先
　　　找好一個對象吧？

海琳：伯母啊，您不必爲我找對象了。我已經——

伯母：有男朋友了？

海琳：嗯(En)——也可以說有了。

伯母：什麼叫"也可以說有了"？有就是有，沒有就是沒有。噢(O)，我知
　　　道了，一定是在大學裡交的朋友吧。咳(Hai)，你們在美國交朋友都是
　　　隨便玩玩的，今天好[iii]，說不定[iv]明天就吹了。談戀愛、結婚可[v]是一
　　　生中的大事啊！怎麼能這麼隨隨便便的呢？

海琳：你怎麼知道我是隨隨便便的呢？我對這些事是很認真的。

| | | | |
|---|---|---|---|
| 正好 | | zhènghǎo | A/MA just at the right time; just right; coincidentally, it just so happens that |
| 戀愛 | 恋爱 | liàn'ài | V/N be in love; romantic love |
| 談戀愛 | 谈恋爱 | tán liàn'ài | VO to get romantically involved, to date |
| 結婚 | 结婚 | jiéhūn | VO to get married, to marry |
| 爲...(而) | 为...(而) | wèi...(ér)... | CV-A. for (the sake/purpose of...) [therefore]... |
| 交朋友 | | jiāo péngyou | VP to make friends |
| 隨便 | 随便 | suíbiàn | ADJ/A casual, informal; do as one pleases; randomly, casually; carelessly |
| 說不定 | 说不定 | shuōbudìng | MA maybe, perhaps |
| 吹了 | | chuī le | IE [colloq.] (relationship) broken up/split; (of a plan) failed/fell through |
| 一生（中） | | yìshēng(zhōng) | N a life-time; all/throughout one's life |
| 認真 | 认真 | rènzhēn | ADJ serious (about sth.) |

i. "我還小呢。" ("I'm still young yet"). 小 means "young". Similarly, 大 means old/older, as in 你多大了？("How old are you?"), or 我比你大 ("I'm older than you").

ii. "我可不想結婚"：可 here is a tonal adverb, providing contrast. The sentence means: "Someone else may want to [get married], but I don't." (See also Note v below for a different use of 可.

iii. "今天好，明天...。" 好 is a casual term for "談戀愛". Here are some more examples:
  他跟王小姐好了，你知道嗎？ He's dating Miss Wang now, did you know?
  我跟他好了三年，後來吹了。 I went steady with him for three years, then we split.

iv. 說不定 (maybe, perhaps), a movable adverb, can occur either before or after the subject or topic. 說不定 is synonymous with "可能" (possibly) or "也許" (maybe, perhaps). Examples:
  他說不定已經來了 (Maybe he's already here).
  說不定我明年會學中文 (Perhaps next year I'll study Chinese).

v. "找對象、結婚可是一生中的大事啊！" The sentence means "[Mind you!] Finding the right marriage partner and getting married is really the big thing in one's life!" 可 here gives a warning or caution tone as in "Mind you!..." or "by any/all means". Here's an example using 可 with the negative 別.
  你可別自作多情啊！ [Mind you!] Don't imagine that he's in love with you.

伯母：那你的男朋友也一樣認真嗎？你可別自作多情啊！聽説現在有不少人都是只談戀愛不結婚的，這樣的人最好跟他一刀兩斷。

海琳：伯母，我知道您關心我，可是談戀愛、結婚是我自己的事，應該讓我自己決定。

伯母：哎呀，你們年輕人都愛這麼説，可是我們老年人比你們見得多，我知道什麼人對你合適。你聽我説，我要給你介紹的這個人是一個研究生，人又聰明，長得又帥，對你再合適也沒有了！你不會不[vi]喜歡他的。我已經跟他家説好了，過幾天就帶你去跟他見面。

海琳：什麼？見面？！

伯母：就是兩個人互相認識認識，別那麼大驚小怪的！

海琳：哎呀伯母，不行不行！

伯母：這有什麼行不行的[vii]？別不好意思。聽我的，沒錯！

---

vi. "你不會不喜歡他的" presents a double negative, which as in English, emphasizes the positive, i.e. 你一定會喜歡他的. This kind of double negative structure is very common in colloquial Chinese. More examples:
　　你不去不行。（=你一定得去。）
　　你的事我不能不管。（=我當然要管。）

vii. 這有什麼行不行的？ (What does this have to do with being OK or not?) This is a rhetorical, suggesting "This situation has nothing to do with being OK or not OK", or "Don't concern yourself with its being OK or not OK." 這 here refers to a prestated/understood topic.
　　*Another example:*
　　A:我真不好意思麻煩你。　B:這有什麼（好意思）不好意思的？

| 自作多情 | | zì zuò duōqíng | IE to imagine that sb. is interested in you |
|---|---|---|---|
| 斷 | 断 | duàn | V (sth.)break/snap |
| 一刀兩斷 | 一刀两断 | yì dāo liǎng duàn | PH. make a clean break (in a relationship) |
| 關心 | 关心 | guānxīn | VO to care about, show concern/care |
| 讓 | 让 | ràng | CV to let, to make, allow |
| 決定 | 决定 | juédìng | V/N to decide; decision |
| 合適 | 合适 | héshì | ADJ be suitable, fitting, appropriate |
| 研究 | | yánjiū | V/N do research; research |
| 研究生 | | yánjiūshēng | N graduate student |
| 長得 | 长得 | zhǎngde | EV [of a person] be (good-looking, tall, thin, etc.) |
| 帥 | 帅 | shuài | ADJ [colloq.] handsome |
| 互相 | | hùxiāng | A each other, one another, mutually |
| 大驚小怪 | 大惊小怪 | dà jīng xiǎo guài | PH alarmed over nothing; make a fuss about nothing |

判斷出以下詞語的意思：

伯父
你聽我說　你听我说
一天到晚
忙得團團轉　忙得团团转

回答問題：
1.海琳爲什麼要到台北來？
2.伯母是一個什麼樣的人？
3.伯母要給海琳介紹一個什麼樣的人？
4.海琳爲什麼不想要伯母給她找對象？
5.伯母對海琳的男朋友有什麼看法？爲什麼？

# 語言結構
### Focusing on Structure

## I. Adding Tone or Vividness with Adjective-Reduplication

As we told you in Lesson One, adjectives, or stative verbs, when reduplicated, bring a vividness to language that is much livelier than the plain form. Remember 大大的，小小的，傻傻的, from Lesson One, as examples of one syllable, reduplicated adjectives. Two-syllable/disyllabic adjectives, when reduplicated, follow an "A A B B (的 )" form (隨隨便便的 ). Since such adjectives (one syllable or two) are already emphatic, adverbs such as 很, 非常, or the suffix 極了, are not used. The following are categories commonly used with reduplication in descriptive language:

> Appearance/looks: 大、小、高、矮、亮、清楚、乾淨、高興
> Senses: 熱、冷、硬、軟、甜、辣
> Colors: 紅、黑、白
> Attitude and Manner: 認真、隨便、馬虎、辛苦、
> 快、慢、熱情、高興、清楚
> Time: 早、晚

Three types of usages are most common. Here are some examples using one and two syllable adjective-reduplication.

1. Describing physical appearances or features, conditions, manners or attitude.
- 他剛才還好好的，怎麼現在就病了？
   He was so healthy a moment ago. So how come he's sick now?
- 對這件事，你怎麼能這麼隨隨便便的呢？
   How can you treat this matter so casually?

2. Stating the extent or result of an action (V+得 +Reduplicated Adjective+的 )
- 她每天都把房間收拾得乾乾淨淨的。
   Everyday she tidies up the rooms nice and clean.

3. Stating the manner or attitude in or with which a person carries out a certain action. Here a reduplicated adjective used with 地 (pronounced de) acts as an adverb and is placed before the action verb.
- 你慢慢(地)說。
   Say it slowly. /Take your time.

- 他買了東西，就高高興興地回家了。
  After shopping, he happily went home/went home happy as a lark.

## II. Softening Tone with Verb Reduplication

Almost opposite to adjective reduplication, which adds emphasis, verbal reduplication aims to deemphasize and make the whole effect milder, very similar to the form "Verb一下" ( 你看一下).　In fact, these two forms are often interchangeable. The reduplicated-verb sets up as A A ＋ Object for monosyllabic verbs and　A B A B ＋ Object for disyllabic verbs. Note that the verbs must be actional and not of the appearing/disappearing, or starting/finishing types. The verbs typically used for reduplication include V-O compounds and some intransitive verbs of motion.

## TWO CAUTIONS:
- Resultative Verb compounds, such as,看見，聽懂，學會 cannot be reduplicated.
- Negated sentences do not use reduplicated forms (我不想看看書 is wrong).

Verb-reduplication is normally used in <u>requests</u>, <u>suggestions</u>, or <u>statements of one's own activity</u> -- realized or planned.

Here are some examples:

A. Monosyllabic Verbs (inserting "一" between the verbs is optional;了 is inserted for past events)

    1.我累了，不想看書了。只想跳跳舞、唱唱歌，或者跟人說說話。
    2.別一天到晚坐在家裡，出去走一走。
    3.我昨天看了看那本書，覺得還不錯。

B. Disyllabic Verbs (here "一" is dropped; 了 is inserted for past events)

    1.我想先熟悉熟悉這裡的情況。
    2.你太累了，應該休息休息。
    3.我到了北京以後，就<u>安排了安排</u>住的地方。(or:安排了一下......)*
    4.我剛才給他<u>介紹了介紹</u>學校的情況。(or:介紹了一下......)*

> * Note that when disyllabic verbs are used to indicate past events,
> V 了 一 下 form is phonologically preferred.

# 辭彙用法
## Word Usage

### Verbs
- 主修：主修英文；你在大學的時候主修什麼？/英文是我的<u>主修</u>(N)。
- 熟悉：熟悉一下這裡的生活；我想熟悉熟悉台灣的情況。/我對那個人（那個地方、那裡的情況）一點也不熟悉。
- 管 ：管孩子；管家；管閒事；你別管我的事！
- 待 ：待在家裡；在中國待過三年；待了幾天；待一段時間
- 安排：安排生活；安排時間；安排工作；我的吃住安排好了\安排得很好；做<u>安排</u>(N)
- 決定：你決定什麼時候走？/我還沒決定/這件事是他決定的。/做<u>決定</u>(N)
- 關心：關心朋友；關心工作；關心一件事；他對找對象的事一點也不關心。
- 長得：長得很高；長得不漂亮；長得像母親
- 斷：筷子斷了；關係(relationship)斷了
- 讓：(to let, allow) 結婚的事應該讓我自己決定。/他不讓我走。/(to make...) 他的話讓我很高興。/別讓他生氣。

### V-O Compounds/Phrases
- 畢業：(從)大學畢業；畢業兩年了；你是哪個學校畢業的？/大學畢業生
- 談戀愛：她正在跟小王談戀愛。/談過幾次戀愛；他們談了三年戀愛了。
- 結婚：小王跟小李結婚了。/你結婚了嗎？/我還沒結婚。/他結過兩次婚。
- 交朋友：交男朋友；交女朋友；交了很多新朋友；喜歡交朋友；他交過一個中國女朋友。

### Resultative Verb Compounds/Phrases
- 說好：我跟他說好今天去。/我跟他說好不去看電影了。/我們沒說好在哪兒見面。

## Adjectives/Adverbs

- 隨便：他很隨便。/他說話很隨便。/他對這件事很隨便。/我隨便看
  了看那本書。
- 認真：做事很認真；學習很認真；工作很認真；認認真真地工作；
  他對這件事很認真。
- 正好：這件衣服不大不小，正好。/你來得正好(just in time)。
- 互相：互相幫助；互相幫忙；互相介紹；互相關心；互相學習
- 合適：這間房子（這個人、這本書）對我很合適。/他做這件事不太
  合適。

## Nouns

- 對象：結婚對象；找對象；給他介紹對象；他已經有對象了。
- 情況：學習情況；生活情況；經濟情況；學校的情況不太好。/
  你的情況怎麼樣？
- 機會：好機會；工作機會；藉這個機會告訴你一件事

## Idioms/Set Phrases

- 自以為是：這個人常常自以為是。/你別自以為是，總覺得你是對的。
- 自作多情：他常常自作多情，總以為別人愛他。/我知道他不愛你，
  你別自作多情。
- 一刀兩斷：你應該跟他一刀兩斷。/我不想跟他結婚，可是也不想跟
  他一刀兩斷。
- 大驚小怪：這件事不奇怪，別大驚小怪的。/這一點點小事，不必大
  驚小怪。

# 句型和習慣用語
## Sentence Patterns and Expressions

**1. 一是......，二是......( for one thing..., for another... )**
- 我沒有去找他，一是我太忙，二是我不知道他住在哪裡。
- 我想學中文，一是我母親是中國人，二是我以後想到中國去工作一段時間。

**Complete:**
- 我沒給他回信，_____
- 他這次到美國來有兩個原因：_____


**2. 該 V 了 ( It's time to...... )**
- 你已經三十多歲了，該結婚了。
  You're already over thirty. It's time for you to get married!
- 你下個禮拜就要出國了。該開始收拾行李了。

**Complete:**
- 時候不早了，_____

**Translate:** It's time for us to go to the airport to pick him up.


**3. 不管......，都 V......( no matter what/who/when/where/how... )**
- 不管我<u>說什麼</u>，他都不聽。No matter what I say, he just won't listen.
- 不管他<u>有沒有</u>錢，我都喜歡他。
- 不管這本書<u>多貴</u>，我都要買。
- 不管你<u>怎麼學</u>，不管你學多少，你都應該認認真真的。

**Complete:**
- 不管 _____，我都（不）_____

**Translate:** No matter what he says, you shouldn't believe him.


**4. Subject 為 (sb. / sth)......（ 而 ）... (Subject is / does... for the sake of/because of/on behalf of ...)**
　　為 is a very flexible word with many meanings, as seen below. In some cases 而 must be used to avoid ambiguity. Compare the following and note how 而 clarifies.
- 我為他工作。(Two interpretations: I'm working for him./ I'm working for his sake/bene-fit.)

- 我爲他而工作。(I for his sake [therefore] work. -- I'm working for his sake.)

   (爲 here indicates cause, 而, meaning "then" or "therefore", suggests effect or result)

*More examples:*

- 她一天到晚爲家事（而）忙得團團轉。

   She is extremely busy all the time because of her housework.

- 我爲學中文（而）到中國去。

**Complete:**

- 他常常爲 _____

**Translate:**

- She has come to America for my sake.


5. ...再...也没有了/不過了 **( Sth. couldn't be better / worse, etc. ... )**

- 這個人又聰明，長得又帥，對你再合適也没有了。This man is both smart and
   handsome.  He is the perfect one for you/No one could be more suitable.

- 要是你願意幫我這個忙，那再好不過了。

**Complete:**

- 這個考試真是 _____

**Complete A's (甲) conversation with B (乙)**

- 甲：明天到我家來吃晚飯，怎麼樣？

   乙：_____


6. 藉...機會 V **( take the opportunity to ...)**

- 他想藉留學中國的機會好好地熟悉一下中國的情況。

   He wants to take the opportunity of studying abroad in China to get familiar with China.

- 他想藉今天吃晚飯的機會把這件事告訴大家。

- 他要在這兒待一段時間，你可以藉這個機會向他學習。

**Complete:**

- 他常常藉上課的機會 _____

**Translate:**

- His aunt wants to take this opportunity to introduce a girl friend to him.

In this lesson you may have found it curious to find Hailin in Taibei having a 'heart-to-heart' chat with her aunt about life and love. Such conversations happen in the United States as well, but more often between mother and daughter. To understand the exchange between Hailin and her aunt, it's useful to keep in mind the still strong influence of the concept of the extended family in China. Certainly in earlier times in China, the extended family (several generations with children residing in a large compound) was considered the ideal. Nowadays, however, a Chinese household will more often consist of a single nuclear family--two parents with children. Of course, because of the 'one child per family' regulation, this usually means only one child, although there are many exceptions, especially in the country-side. Moreover, in today's China, because of the economic necessity for both spouses to work, one often finds the grandparents sharing the same household with their children,  and helping out with family chores, such as baby-sitting. In such situations, the grandparents, because of their seniority, often exercise an advisory role over family affairs. Even in cases where grandparents, or other relatives, such as aunts and uncles, have their own residences, they can still play an important role in managing the affairs of a Chinese family. The marriage of the children is not only mom and dad's worry but the entire family's concern. Therefore, not only will the grandparents and parents offer un-asked for advice to the young man or the young woman, but even uncles and aunts also feel it their duty to 'get in the act.' This is another reflection of the importance not only of the basic family unit but, in a real sense, of the 'extended family' in China. In today's China, despite the many changes that have occurred over the past half-century, the family, not the individual, continues, as in the past, to be the vital social unit around which the entire fabric of society is built.

So it's not at all strange, given these considerations, to find 伯母 freely giving advice about dating and marriage to Hailin. Hailin, coming from American culture, is a bit put off by this, and this is also natural and expected. On this trip to Taiwan, she'll have to learn not only about Chinese language but also about Chinese behavior and customs.

## 第一部分：單句

請你們聽下面的句子。每個句子的意思是什麼？請在三個選擇中選出一句來。
Listen to the recorded statements. Circle the sentence from the three choices which is closest in meaning to the statement heard.

1. (a)要是你不喜歡這個工作，你就隨便做做吧。
   (b)這個工作你喜歡也好，不喜歡也好，你都應該認真地做。
   (c)我不知道你到底喜不喜歡這個工作。

2. (a)他在這所大學待了很長的時間了，應該趕快畢業。
   (b)他是六年前從這所大學畢業的。
   (c)他畢業以後應該留在這所大學教書。

3. (a)教書是非常辛苦的工作。
   (b)教書這種工作一點兒也不辛苦。
   (c)教書是很容易的工作。

4. (a)她結婚以前不必工作，生活非常舒服。
   (b)她結婚以後，生活舒服得不得了。
   (c)她結婚以後，天天為家裡的事忙得團團轉。

5. (a)小張和他女朋友快結婚了。
   (b)小張剛交了一個新的女朋友。
   (c)小張和他女朋友不在一起了。

6. (a)王先生今天要帶他的對象來我家吃飯。
   (b)今天吃晚飯的時候，我想給王先生介紹個女朋友。
   (c)王先生想在吃晚飯的時候給我介紹對象。

## 第二部分：對話

第一遍:下面是海琳伯父、伯母的對話。請你們聽懂這個對話的大意，然後回答問題。
First Listening: Listen to the recorded dialogue between Hailin's aunt and uncle. Try to get a general idea of what it is about. After you listen, answer the question.

<u>問題</u>：伯父和伯母在談些什麼？
 a)給他們的兒子找對象的事　　　　b)給海琳介紹對象的事

第二遍:請你們讀下面的句子。然後把這個對話再聽一次。聽完後，看看這些句子說得對不對。
Second Listening: Read the following statements. Then listen to the dialogue again. After you listen, decide whether the statements are true or false.

_____1.伯母想給海琳介紹一個男朋友。
_____2.德生不喜歡現在的女朋友，他想找一個新的對象。
_____3.伯父、伯母都覺得海琳跟德生很合適。
_____4.伯父不喜歡伯母管年輕人談戀愛的事。

第三遍:請你們聽第三遍，然後從下面每組句子中，選出一句對的來。
Third Listening: Listen to the dialogue a third time. Then circle the correct statement from each of the following pairs.

1. a)德生是伯母同學的兒子。
　　b)德生是伯母兒子的同學。

2. a)德生本來有一個女朋友，可是已經吹了。
　　b)德生剛找到一個新對象。

3. a)伯母覺得德生對海琳很合適，所以想把他介紹給海琳。
　　b)伯母想把德生介紹給海琳，因為德生要伯母幫他找對象。

4. a)伯母說年輕人不喜歡自己找對象。
　　b)伯母說年輕人不知道找什麼人結婚合適。

5. a)伯父覺得伯母不應該管別人的閒事。
　　b)伯父覺得現在的人談戀愛很隨便。

6. a)伯父跟伯母是自己認識、戀愛，然後結婚的。
　　b)伯父跟伯母是別人介紹認識，然後才結婚的。

7. a)伯父說父母給孩子找的對象多半不錯。
　　b)伯父說現在的年輕人多半不喜歡父母替他們找對象。

I.填入適當的詞語:

1.原因：我今天沒上課的原因_____。/他沒_____有幾個原因。

2.主修：小王在哥大主修_____。/你的主修是_____還是_____？

3.熟悉：我很熟悉_____。/我_____這裡的情況不太熟悉。/你到了

　　　那裡，先熟悉一下_____。

4.情況：美國現在的_____情況不太好。/你這幾個月的情況_____？

5.能幹：他是_____。/他真_____！做事做得又快又好。

6.安排：安排_____；把_____安排_____很好；你下個星

　　　期天 _____安排？

7.認真：他很_____學了一年中文。/小王學中文_____

　　　_____。/他_____什麼事都很認真。

8.互相：互相（不）_____；_____互相幫助（關心）。


II.改寫句子:

1.我已經好幾年沒有回國了，應該回去看看。（該……了）


2.對我來説，他長得帥不帥沒關係，我還是喜歡他。（不管……都……）


3.我的朋友出國了；這段時間我住在他那裡。（藉……機會V……）


4.他寫字寫得慢得不得了！（再……也沒有了！）

5.我今天要去跟對象見面，所以穿得漂漂亮亮的。（爲......而......）

6.我到中國去是因爲我想學中文，我也想熟悉熟悉中國的情況。
（一是......，二是......）

III.<u>造句</u> (Make sentences with the following):

自作多情；自以爲是；一刀兩斷；大驚小怪

IV.(A)<u>用重疊式改寫句子</u> (Rewrite the phrases using the reduplicated form). (Note: 了 should be inserted for a past event; 一 is optional for monosyllabic verbs but should be left out for diasyllabic verbs and for past actions.)

1.我剛才看<u>了一下書</u>。　　　　　　＿＿＿＿＿＿＿＿＿＿＿＿＿

2.你太累了，<u>休息一下</u>吧。　　　　＿＿＿＿＿＿＿＿＿＿＿＿＿

3.你能不能給我<u>介紹一下</u>這裡的情況？　＿＿＿＿＿＿＿＿＿＿＿＿＿

4.我昨天跟他<u>見了一下</u>面。　　　　　＿＿＿＿＿＿＿＿＿＿＿＿＿

5.我想<u>熟悉一下</u>這裡的情況。　　　　＿＿＿＿＿＿＿＿＿＿＿＿＿

6.他爲我<u>安排了一下</u>住的地方。　　　＿＿＿＿＿＿＿＿＿＿＿＿＿

7.你得<u>關心一下</u>你自己的事了。　　　＿＿＿＿＿＿＿＿＿＿＿＿＿

(B)<u>用否定+否定式改寫句子</u> (Rewrite the sentence using double negative forms)

例 (Example):這件事我一定要管。--->這件事我<u>不管不行</u>。/這件事我<u>不能不管</u>。

1.我父母説我<u>得學中文</u>。　　　　　　＿＿＿＿＿＿＿＿＿＿＿＿＿

2.你想説好中文，<u>就得天天練習</u>。　　＿＿＿＿＿＿＿＿＿＿＿＿＿

3.你見了他，就<u>一定會喜歡他的</u>。　　＿＿＿＿＿＿＿＿＿＿＿＿＿

5.這本書再好也沒有了，所以<u>我一定要買</u>。　＿＿＿＿＿＿＿＿＿＿＿＿＿

6.中國人説，<u>父母的話當然要聽</u>。　　＿＿＿＿＿＿＿＿＿＿＿＿＿

7.學中文<u>一定得有一本字典</u>(zìdiǎn:dictionary)。　＿＿＿＿＿＿＿＿＿＿＿

## 一個母親的看法

　　現在的年輕人談戀愛真是太隨便了！今天跟這個<u>好</u>1，明天又<u>約</u>2那個出去。好的時候兩個人都會説："我不能沒有你！我只愛你一個！我願意<u>爲你而死</u>3！"可是過幾天也許<u>同樣的話</u>4就會對另外一個人説了。從前孩子的<u>婚事</u>5都是<u>父母包辦</u>6，這當然不好。可是現在的年輕人自己找對象是不是就真的好了呢？如果好的話，爲什麼<u>離婚</u>7的人越來越多了呢？很多年輕人<u>開始</u>8都不願聽父母的話，可是後來<u>發現</u>9父母的話很多都是對的。<u>拿我的兒子來説吧</u>10，他<u>前前後後</u>11已經談了四次戀愛了！每一次他開始都説他的女朋友<u>怎麼怎麼好</u>12，可是後來<u>一個一個都吹了</u>13。我跟他説，如果<u>見一個就愛一個</u>14，那麼<u>永遠</u>15不會真的愛一個人。找對象也不能只看長得漂亮不漂亮，最重要的是她的<u>心</u>16好不好，當然也得看看兩個人的<u>家庭</u>17是不是合適。我告訴他，他的第一個女朋友雖然沒有另外几個漂亮，但她才是<u>真心</u>18愛他。可是我儿子就是不聽！還是跟她<u>分手了</u>19。他總是説："<u>不管</u>20我找的對象對不對、好不好，都是我自己的事，我不要別人<u>管</u>21。"
......可是前幾天他突然對我説："媽媽，也許你説得對：找對象不應該找<u>臉</u>22，應該找心！"

<u>請寫出畫有底綫的詞語的意思</u> (Give the meaning of the underlined words/phrases):

1.＿＿＿＿＿＿　　2.＿＿＿＿＿＿　　3.＿＿＿＿＿＿　　4.＿＿＿＿＿＿

5.＿＿＿＿＿＿　　6.＿＿＿＿＿＿　　7.＿＿＿＿＿＿　　8.＿＿＿＿＿＿

9.＿＿＿＿＿＿　　10.＿＿＿＿＿＿　　11.＿＿＿＿＿＿　　12.＿＿＿＿＿＿

13.＿＿＿＿＿＿　　14.＿＿＿＿＿＿　　15.＿＿＿＿＿＿　　16.＿＿＿＿＿＿

17.＿＿＿＿＿＿　　18.＿＿＿＿＿＿　　19.＿＿＿＿＿＿　　20.＿＿＿＿＿＿

21.＿＿＿＿＿＿　　22.＿＿＿＿＿＿

哪一句對？

1a.這位母親覺得年輕人不應該很早就談戀愛。
1b.這位母親覺得談戀愛應該認真一點。

2a.她說年輕人找對象的時候應該聽聽父母的看法。
2b.她說年輕人自己找對象沒有父母包辦好。

3a.她的兒子不聽她的話，所以女朋友都跟他吹了。
3b.她的兒子交過的女朋友裡有一個她覺得不錯。

4a.母親覺得找對象不應該看長得好不好。
4b.母親覺得兩個人的家庭合適不合適最重要。

5a.兒子覺得父母說得都不對，所以不願意聽。
5b.兒子覺得不管別人說得對不對，都應該讓他自己決定自己的事。

# 口語練習

I.用所給的句型回答:
A:你的男朋友對你到底是不是真心的，如果不是，我看你最好趕快跟他吹了吧。
B:（不管......,都......）

A:我們先去台北，然後去香港 (Xiānggǎng:HongKong)，最後到北京，怎麼樣？
B:（再......也沒有了！）

A:這是我給你姐姐買的衣服，不知道她喜歡不喜歡？
B:（再......也沒有了；不會不......的）

II.情景會話:介紹男朋友/女朋友
假設你的親戚或者好朋友想給你介紹一個女/男朋友。你先聽他/她介紹那個人的情況。然後，你也問一些你關心的問題。(兩人一組練習)

III.談看法：請你談談你對找對象的看法。你覺得找對象的時候父母的看法重要不重要？

# 寫作練習

1.談看法

　　看完上面的閱讀短文《一個母親的看法》以後，你有什麼看法？你覺得那位母親說的對嗎？爲什麼？你有什麼例子？

2.看圖習作

"小王的終身大事"

（你可以這樣開始）：小王是一個中國人，他已經二十五了，可是還沒有對象，所以親友們都爲他着急。......

有用的詞彙和短語：

喜酒 "wedding wine"--the wedding banquet

請親戚朋友 to invite relatives and friends

參加婚禮 [cānjiā hūnlǐ] to attend the wedding ceromony

祝你們早得貴子 [zhù nǐmen zǎo dé guìzǐ] May you have a child soon!

# "醫生，我哪兒都不舒服"

## 一看病一

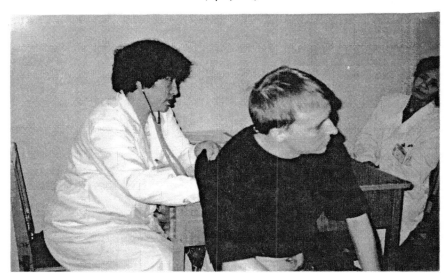

第四課

| Situation | Structure | Culture |
|-----------|-----------|---------|
| 語言情景 | 語言結構 | 文化介紹 |

Our scene shifts to 北京 where we find 大為 settled in but not quite used to his new environment. He gets sick and you can take the opportunity to learn some useful language about seeing a doctor, having symptoms of illness, etc.

Look out for these new structures:
- using Verb -起來 to express the start of a new situation;
- using Verb-着 + another verbal phrase to express two simultaneous actions.

Culturally, you will learn something about Chinese attitudes towards medicine (中國人看病和吃藥).

# "醫生，我哪兒都不舒服"
## --看病--

　　　大爲到了北京以後，沒有幾天就生病了。原因是他剛到一個新地方，還不適應這裡的環境和天氣，結果就開始打噴嚏、咳嗽。大爲想，大概是感冒了，不算什麼病，過几天就會好的。可是病一點也沒好：不但咳嗽咳得越來越厲害，而且頭也疼起來了。這兩天不知道怎麼搞的[i]，肚子也不舒服了，只好到學校的醫務室來看病。

醫生：你哪兒不舒服啊？

大爲：醫生，我哪兒都不舒服。前幾天好像着了一點涼，開始[ii]只是咳嗽，可是咳着咳着，頭也疼起來了。昨天又開始瀉肚子——哎喲，我的頭怎麼這麼疼？也有一點燙，大概是發燒了。

醫生：我來給你檢查檢查。張開嘴，"啊"--

大爲：啊--

醫生：好了。來，量一下體溫。......你是發燒了，三十八度五。

大爲：怪不得這麼難受！

醫生：......解開衣服扣子，深呼吸——呼氣——再吸氣——呼氣。好了，穿好衣服吧。還好，問題不大。

大爲：醫生，我的肚子也不太好。今天早上一吃東西就吐，連喝牛奶都不行。現在我真是一點力氣也沒有了。

---

i. 不知道怎麼搞的 is an idiomatic expression meaning "somehow or other," or "who knows how it happened."

ii. "開始只是咳嗽..." 開始 here is a short form for 開始的時候 "at first", "in the beginning." Contrast it with 開始咳嗽 in which 開始 means "start" ("start to cough").

| 醫 | 医 | yī | V to treat (a patient, an ailment); BF medical |
| 醫生 | 医生 | yīshēng | N (medical) doctor, physician |
| 生病 | | shēng//bìng | VO to fall ill, get sick |
| 適應 | 适应 | shìyìng | V/ADJ to get adjusted to; accustomed to |
| 環境 | 环境 | huánjìng | N environment |
| 結果 | 结果 | jiéguǒ | MA/N consequently, end up being...; result |
| 感冒 | | gǎnmào | N/V flu, cold; to have a cold/flu |
| 打噴嚏 | 打喷嚏 | dǎ pēntì | VO to sneeze |
| 咳嗽 | | késou | V/N to cough; cough |
| 算 | | suàn | V to count; to be considered as |
| 病 | | bìng | N/V disease, ailment; to be sick |
| 不但...而且 | | búdàn...érqiě | MA not only..., but also... |
| 咳 | | ké | V cough |
| 厲害 | 厉害 | lìhai | ADJ severe |
| 疼 | | téng | V (a body part) to ache, hurt, pain |
| 醫務室 | 医务室 | yīwùshì | N clinic, medical office (of a school, company) |
| 着涼 | 着凉 | zháo liáng | VO to catch cold |
| 瀉肚(子) | 泻肚(子) | xiè dù(zi) | VO to have diarrhea (肚子, belly) |
| 燙 | 烫 | tàng | ADJ be scalding hot, hotter than normal |
| 發燒 | 发烧 | fā//shāo | VO to have a fever |
| 檢查 | 检查 | jiǎnchá | V/N to examine, inspect; checkup, inspection |
| 張嘴 | 张嘴 | zhāng zuǐ | VO to open the mouth |
| 量 | | liáng | V to measure (temperature, length, etc.) |
| 體溫 | 体温 | tǐwēn | N body temperature |
| 度 | | dù | M degree (of temperature, angle, etc.) |
| 怪不得 | | guàibude | IE no wonder... (= to 難怪/难怪) |
| 難受 | 难受 | nánshòu | ADJ sad, unbearable, intolerable |
| 解開 | 解开 | jiěkāi | V to untie, unfasten |
| 扣 | | kòuzi | N (clothes) button |
| 呼 | | hū | V to exhale |
| 吸 | | xī | V inhale |
| 氣 | 气 | qì | N air, gas, vapor |
| 吐 | | tǔ | V to spit, spit something out |
| 吐 | | tù | V to vomit, throw up |
| 力氣 | 力气 | lìqi | N. physical strength |

醫生：可能是你剛來，水土不服。另外，你是不是吃了什麼不乾淨的東西？

大爲：沒有啊，這幾天就是吃了點水果、肉包子、雞蛋、涼麵什麼的。喝的也就是點牛奶、咖啡、汽水、自來水。

醫生：你吃東西得注意衛生，就是新鮮的水果，也得削了皮或者洗乾淨了再吃。另外，自來水也不夠衛生，不要隨便喝。

大爲：我以前在美國吃水果都是連皮吃的，而且天天都喝自來水，從來沒問題。

醫生：美國是美國，中國是中國，一個地方跟一個地方不一樣嘛。你得適應這裡的條件才行。這樣吧，拿着這個藥方去拿藥。這幾天多喝水，少吃肉和生、冷的東西。別忘了吃藥，也別到處跑。在家好好休息兩天。

大爲：糟糕！我今天有課，明天還有一個考試呢。

醫生：你發着燒怎麼去上課考試啊？別拿身體開玩笑。我給你開一個證明，你跟老師請兩天假就行了。

大爲：那好吧。唉(Ài)！早不病晚不病，偏偏<sup>iii</sup>要考試的時候病——真要命<sup>iv</sup>！

---

回答問題：
1. 大爲爲什麼剛到北京不久就生病了？
2. 大爲什麼地方不舒服？
3. 醫生說爲什麼大爲肚子不好？
4. 醫生要大爲吃東西的時候注意些什麼？
5. 爲什麼醫生要給大爲開證明？
6. 你剛到一個新地方的時候會不會覺得有什麼地方不舒服？病了你會怎麼辦？

---

iii. 早不 + verb 晚不 + verb expresses that the verbal action does not occur at the right time (lit. "neither early nor late") but at just (偏偏) the *wrong* time. See *Sentence Patterns and Expressions*, for more on this usage. 偏 or 偏偏 is an adverb expressing that a situation or a person is contrary to one's expectations or wishes, roughly corresponding to English "but it just happened that..." or "[someone] just choose to ...." Here are some examples:
　　我去看他，可是他偏偏不在家。I went see him, but he just happened to be out.
　　他不要我去，我偏要去。He doesn't want me to go, [but] I will go [anyway]!
　　我們正想出去玩兒，可是偏偏下起雨來! It started to rain just when we were about to go out!

iv. 真要命 is an exclamation used to express frustration, anger, disappointment, dissatisfaction, meaning "(Such and such is) so awful!" or "It drives me crazy!" or "It's killing me".
　　這裡夏天的天氣真要命！The weather here in the summer is killing me!
　　他什麼都不吃，真要命！He doesn't eat anything; it drives me crazy!

| | | | |
|---|---|---|---|
| 水土不服 | | shuǐtǔ bù fú | PH negative physical reactions caused by a new environment ("The water and soil don't agree with you.") |
| 另外 | | lìngwài | MA in addition, besides |
| 包子 | | bāozi | N steamed stuffed bun (肉包子, bun stuffed with meat) |
| 麵 | 面 | miàn | N noodles; flour, dough |
| 自來水 | 自来水 | zìláishuǐ | N tap water |
| 注意 | | zhùyì | V to pay attention to, watch |
| 衛生 | 卫生 | wèishēng | ADJ sanitary; sanitation; hygienic, hygiene |
| 新鮮 | 新鲜 | xīnxiān | ADJ fresh |
| 削 | | xiāo | V to scrape, peel, pare |
| 皮 | | pí | N skin; leather |
| 或者 | | huòzhě | CONJ or (as in either...or...) |
| 洗 | | xǐ | V to wash |
| 乾淨 | 干净 | gānjìng | ADJ be clean (洗乾淨, RV wash clean) |
| 連 | 连 | lián | CV including, with.....included |
| 嘛 | | ma | p (Particle suggesting obviousness) |
| 條件 | 条件 | tiáojiàn | N condition, term |
| 藥方 | 药方 | yàofāng | N prescription |
| 吃藥 | 吃药 | chī yào | VO to take medicine (orally); (藥, medicine, remedy) |
| 到處 | 到处 | dàochù | PW everywhere |
| 開 | 开 | kāi | V to make out (a list, prescription, check) |
| 證明 | 证明 | zhèngmíng | V/N to prove, certify; certifying letter |
| 請假 | 请假 | qǐngjià | VO to ask for a leave of absence |
| 偏偏 | | piānpiān | MA (see *Notes* and *Sentence Patterns and Expressions*) |
| 真要命 | | zhēn yàomìng | IE It's awful! It drives me crazy! |

# 語言結構
## Focusing on Structure

## I. Using V+起來 "V+qǐlái" to express the beginning of an action/new state

起來 is often attached to an action verb or an adjective to express a newly occurring event or state, translating as "start to..." or "start to get/become...." However, its usage differs from 開始 ("begin","start") in that 開始 indicates the starting point of a particular activity or event, while 起來 implies a spontaneous transition or change from a previous event or state to a new event or state. In other words, -起來 depends on a presupposed or assumed situation--stated or implied. -起來 applies to a wider range of verbs and adjectives, in addition to activity verbs (e.g.學中文，跑，笑，興奮，漂亮). 開始 sometimes co-occurs with 起來.

Keep in mind that 起來 should be split when used with a V-O compound, e.g. V起 Object 來 (談起話來).

Examples:

他們見面後沒有幾天就談起戀愛來了。They got romantically involved shortly after they met.

她剛才很生氣，現在高興起來了。She was mad a moment ago, but now she's cheering up.

天氣（開始）熱起來了。The weather is warming up now.

她現在不好看，過幾年會漂亮起來的。She's plain now, but in a few years she will turn pretty.

## II. Using 着 to express "ongoing state" and simultaneous actions

着 is often used with verbs to express the durative/ongoing state of an action or the ongoing physical presence of somebody or something.

我這幾天正看着那本書。 I have been reading that book these few days.

他在屋子裡坐着。 He is sitting in the room.

桌子上放着幾本書。 On the desk lay several books.

(我)走着走着，突然下起雨來。 As I was walking, it suddenly started to rain.

In addition, 着 is also commonly used in a V1+着V2 structure to express two simultaneous actions, i.e. two actions going on at the same time with the V-着 as backgrounding or accompaniment of the main action or event. Here are some examples:

他喜歡看着電視吃晚飯。 He likes to watch TV while eating his dinner.

你怎麼開着燈睡覺？ Why do you sleep with the light on?

別躺着看書。 Don't read lying down.

我每天走着去學校。I go to school on foot everyday/I walk to school everyday.

# 辭彙用法
## Word Usage

## Verbs
- 適應：適應天氣；適應環境；適應新生活；適應要求；適應得很快；
  對中國的生活習慣不適應
- 檢查：檢查行李；檢查身體；把行李檢查一下；檢查完了
- 吐 (to spit)：把你嘴里的東西吐出來；吐在地上
- 吐 (to vomit)：今天我一吃東西就想吐。／我今天吐了兩次了。
- 開：開藥方；給我開一個證明；證明開好了。
- 注意：注意衛生；請注意看牌子上寫的字。／你說什麼？我沒注意聽。
- 削：削水果皮；削鉛筆 (qiānbǐ: pencil)；水果削好了。／削了皮再吃。
- 休息：休息一段時間；好好休息休息；休息得不夠
- 量：量體溫；量身高；量體重；量一量這間屋子有多大；量得不對
- 算：感冒算不算病？／中文不算太難學。／他算我們班上長得最高的。
- 洗：洗衣服；洗手；把手洗乾淨；這件衣服洗得乾淨不乾淨？／洗得乾淨洗不
  乾淨？

## V-O Compounds/Phrases
- 生病：他（生）病了；生過一次大病；沒生過病；常常生病
- 吃藥：吃中藥；吃西藥；飯前吃藥；飯後吃藥；四小時吃一次藥；吃錯藥了
- 看病：今年看了三次病；沒看過病；到醫務室去看病
- 發燒：你發燒了。／發了兩次燒；發高燒；發燒發得很厲害
- 着涼：着了一點涼；外頭天冷，小心着涼。
- 請假：跟老師請假；替他請假；請病假；請事假；請過一次假；請兩天假

## Resultative Verb Compounds/Phrases
- 解開：解開衣服；解開扣子；把衣服解開；把扣子解開；解得開\解不開

## Adjectives
- 新鮮：新鮮的水果；新鮮的空氣；新鮮的事；空氣很新鮮。／
  這杯牛奶不新鮮。
- 厲害：病得很厲害；咳嗽咳得很厲害；頭疼得厲害；想家想得很厲害

## Nouns
- 衛生：環境衛生；個人衛生；衛生習慣；這個飯館的菜很不衛生。(Adj.)
- 環境：學習環境；工作環境；學校的環境；學中文的環境；環境很好
- 證明：工作證明；醫生證明；學校給我開了一個證明，證明我是這裡的
  學生。(V)

## Coverbs
- 連：蘋果可以連皮（一塊）吃。／買書的時候，我連錄音帶（lùyīndài, audio
  tape）一起買了。

# 句型和習慣用語
## Sentence Patterns and Expressions

**1. V 着 V 着, V/Adj. 起(O)來 (While..., ...started to ...)**

- 這幾天我老咳嗽。咳着咳着，頭也疼起來了。
  These few days I've coughed all the time. As I coughed, my head began to hurt.
- 我們走着走着，突然下起雨來。
  While we were walking,  it suddenly started to rain.
- 她說着說着，_____
- 他們常常一起_____ ，_____ ，就談起戀愛來了。
- While he was sleeping, he suddenly burst into laughter.

**2. V1 着 V2 (Sb. is/has ....[accompaniment or means] while doing sth. )**

- 你發着燒考試, 怎麼考得好？
  How can you possibly do well on your test if you have a fever while taking it.
- 我需要新鮮空氣，所以要開着窗戶睡覺。I need fresh air, so I keep the windows open
  while I sleep/so I sleep with the window open.
- 我（不）喜歡 _____看書。
- When having a party (聚會, jùhuì) Americans often eat food standing.

**3. 没(duration of time)就 V 了 ( sb.\ sth. .... in less than [time] )**

- 他到了美國以後，沒兩天就病了。
  He got sick just a few days after he arrived in the U.S.
- 他學中文，學了沒幾天就決定不學了。
  He studied Chinese but quit after a few days.
- 他上了飛機，_____
- He went to Taipei and became very familiar with the environment there in less than a
  month.

**4.** 不但......, 而且（也）......(not only ... but also...)

- 他不但咳嗽咳得越來越厲害，而且頭也疼起來了。

- 他不但（不）熟悉美國的情況，而且也（不）熟悉中國的情況。

- 我不但（不）_____，而且也（不）_____ _____

- I went to China not only to study Chinese but also to acquaint myself with Chinese culture.

**5.** ......得......才行 (Sb. has got to do ...before...)

- 你得適應這裡的條件才行。

  You've got to get adjusted to the conditions here.

- 飛機場離我家很遠，我得坐出租車去才行。

- 我已經有對象了，但是現在還不能結婚，因為我得 _____

- If you want to get better sooner, you've got to rest more.

**6.** 早不......晚不......，偏偏在...的時候V (Sb. does/did sth. at the worst time)

- 他早不來晚不來，偏偏在我要睡覺了的時候來了！(真要命！) He didn't come at a good time but chose to come just when I was about to go to sleep! Damn it!

- 爲什麼你早不說晚不說，偏偏在這個時候說？

  You didn't tell me all this time. How come you've chosen now to finally let me know?

- 她早不打電話來，晚不打電話來，_____

- Why do you choose to apply for studying abroad at the time when your family needs you?

**7.** 就是......，也......（ **even if..., sb/sth....** ）

- 你就是給他錢，他也不會願意做這件事的。

  He won't do this even if you give him money.

- 你就是不能來，也請先給我打個電話。

  Please give me a call even if you can't come.

- 考試 ＿＿＿＿＿＿＿＿＿＿＿＿＿＿＿＿＿＿＿＿＿＿＿，你也得好好地準備。

- You must go even if you don't want to.

**8.** 不知道怎麼搞的，......（ **who knows how it happened...;  I've no idea ...; somehow...** ）

- 不知道怎麼搞的，我這幾天總是睡不好覺。

  I don't know why these days I haven't been sleeping well.

- 不知道怎麼搞的，他今天特別高興。

- 不知道怎麼搞的，＿＿＿＿＿＿＿＿＿＿＿＿＿＿＿＿＿＿＿＿＿＿＿＿＿＿

- I don't know why but I just can't write these characters well.

When a Chinese person gets sick, the choices of medical treatment are varied: he can take his choice of Western medicine and get a response familiar to us, or see a Chinese doctor and perhaps get some herbal treatment (中藥, herbal/Chinese medicine), or see acupuncturist or a massage specialist, or even mix and match from among the above. The Chinese attitude is eclectic and practical, typically Chinese. This does not mean that Chinese are frivolous about choosing doctors or getting medical treatment. It just means that the view is: if it works, use it. For Chinese, the various kinds of treatment available are not mutually exclusive. It is not surprising to find a Chinese doctor of western medicine prescribing both Chinese and western medicines for the same patient.

Many Chinese believe that western medicine is good for life-threatening illnesses, such as heart desease or cancer, etc., that need strong and immediate treatment. But they also feel that western medicine tends to produce side effects which may bring on other, unwelcome problems. Thus, they rely more on Chinese medicines for minor illnesses because such medicines produce very few undesirable side effects.

Lots of Chinese opt for holistic treatment, that is, a medical response that seeks to treat the whole body rather than zero in on a particular organ. So if you have appendicitis, a Western doctor would naturally operate while a Chinese doctor might try to reverse the infection with herbs, which may include such things as powdered deer antlers, rhino horns or other exotic ingredients. Herbal medicines are fairly safe, with relatively few side effects and often remarkably effective.

The concern that Chinese have for a friend's well-being includes a concern for the health of their friends. If a friend is ill, a Chinese will not hesitate to give advice and quite often will offer the sick person their own medicine or even go to the trouble of getting medicine from the pharmacy. If you're the beneficiary of such an offer, don't decline it. A refusal would indicate distrust. If you're offered medicine by a

Chinese friend, accept it in friendship. Naturally, you don't have to actually take the medicine. Maybe it's a good idea to assemble your own medical kit filled with your favorites before you leave and bring it along. You never know when 水土不服 will strike!

# 第四課聽力練習

## 第一部分：單句

請你們聽下面的句子。每個句子的意思是什麼？請在三個選擇中選出一句來。
Listen to the recorded statements. Circle the sentence from the three choices which is closest in meaning to the statement heard.

1. (a)他很快地就把這件事安排好了。
   (b)他還要兩天才能把這件事安排好。
   (c)他兩天前就把這件事安排好了。

2. (a)他吃了藥以後覺得舒服多了。
   (b)他吃了藥以後身體更不舒服了。
   (c)他吃了藥以後病就好了。

3. (a)大家都知道這個人爲什麼請長假。
   (b)誰都知道這個人爲什麼只請了幾天的假。
   (c)我不明白這個人爲什麼只工作了幾天就請假。

4. (a)北部和南部的天氣不一樣。
   (b)南部的天氣沒有北部的熱。
   (c)北部的天氣跟南部的一樣熱。

5. (a)你工作得這麼辛苦，該休息了。
   (b)你不應該在工作最忙的時候休息。
   (c)你最好不要在早上和晚上休息。

6. (a)你應該吃吃這種水果。
   (b)你怎麼連這種水果也沒吃過？
   (c)不管你吃沒吃過這種水果，你都應該聽說過。

## 第二部分：短文

第一遍:請你們聽懂這篇短文的大意，然後回答問題。

First Listening: Listen to the recorded story. Try to get a general idea of what it is about. After you listen, answer the question.

問題：這個人為什麼有兩天沒去上課？

    a)因為她的朋友病了

    b)因為她想待在宿舍裡睡覺

    c)因為她病得很厲害

第二遍:請你們讀下面的句子，然後把這篇短文一段一段地再聽一次。聽完每一段後，看看這些句子說得對不對。

Second Listening: Read the following statements. Then listen to the story paragraph by paragraph and pay attention to details. After you listen to each paragraph, decide whether the statements about it are true or false.

第一段：

    ____ 1.這個人因為喝了太多牛奶，所以肚子不舒服。

    ____ 2.這個人不知道她為什麼生病。

    ____ 3.這個人是在上課的時候，突然覺得不舒服的。

    ____ 4.第二天早上，她喝了牛奶就覺得好多了。

第二段：

    ____ 1.她是自己到醫務室去看病的。

    ____ 2.醫生要她在家吃藥休息。

    ____ 3.她的請假條是她的朋友幫她寫的。

    ____ 4.她生病待在宿舍的時候，天天都緊張得睡不着覺。

# 第四課練習
## 辭彙；句型；語法

I.填入適當的詞語：

1.適應：他剛到中國的時候_____那裡的天氣不適應；不過，他適應
　　　　_____很快。

2.檢查：對不起，上飛機以前我們得檢查一下你的_____。/我剛檢查過
　　　　_____，醫生說我沒問題。/他怎麼檢查_____這麼慢？檢查
　　　　_____一個多鐘頭了還沒有檢查_____。

3.休息：你太累了，該_____。/他沒看病吃藥，只休息_____兩
　　　　天，就好了。

4.吐(tǔ)/吐(tù)：他不舒服，一吃東西就_____，今天_____三次了。/哎
　　　　呀，你吃錯藥了，趕快吐_____。

5.注意：吃東西得注意_____。/上課的時候，你得注意聽_____。

6.算：他說頭疼_____病。/他在我們學校算_____的學生。

7.洗：她在洗_____。/你得把_____洗乾淨再吃東西。/這件
　　　衣服我已經_____，還是_____乾淨。

8.生病/病：上個月他_____一次病，_____了一個星期才好。/這種_____
　　　很不容易醫好。/你今年_____過嗎？/他_____得怎麼樣了？

9.新鮮：我喜歡吃新鮮_____。/我得出去呼吸一點_____。/
　　　這杯牛奶已經_____了，喝了一定會_____。/你說
　　　的事情我早聽說過了，一點也_____。

10.環境：你_____不_____那裡的環境？/我們學校的_____環
　　　境很不錯。

II.<u>寫出句子的意思</u>(Write your interpretation of each sentence in Chinese)：

1.你怎麼早不去晚不去，偏偏要在我生病的時候去？

　　　意思是：＿＿＿＿＿＿＿＿＿＿＿＿＿＿＿＿＿＿＿＿＿＿

2.你是你，我是我！

　　　意思是：＿＿＿＿＿＿＿＿＿＿＿＿＿＿＿＿＿＿＿＿＿＿

3.你到中國去留學，<u>就得適應那裡的環境才行</u>。

　　　意思是：＿＿＿＿＿＿＿＿＿＿＿＿＿＿＿＿＿＿＿＿＿＿

4.<u>我大學畢業沒幾天</u>就找到了一個工作。

　　　意思是：＿＿＿＿＿＿＿＿＿＿＿＿＿＿＿＿＿＿＿＿＿＿

5.這種病，你就是不吃藥也會好的。

　　　意思是：＿＿＿＿＿＿＿＿＿＿＿＿＿＿＿＿＿＿＿＿＿＿

6.他不但常常自以為是，而且也愛自作多情。

　　　意思是：＿＿＿＿＿＿＿＿＿＿＿＿＿＿＿＿＿＿＿＿＿＿

III.<u>用 "着" 的用法改寫句子</u>(rewrite the sentences using 着)：

1.他一邊吃飯，一邊看電視。(V着V)

2.你開車的時候別說話。(V着V)

3.他<u>在看書的時候</u>睡着了。(V着V着)

4.剛學中文的時候她覺得中文很難，<u>慢慢地</u>就覺得不難了。(V着V着)

5.我每天去上學的時候都是騎車去。(V着V)

6.你吃飯的時候怎麼總是站着？(V着V)

7.她不知怎麼搞的，先是哭[kū:cry]，後來又笑了。(V着V着,...起來)

IV.下面句子裡應該用 "開始" 還是 "起來"

     (Which should be used:開始 or起來)？

1.我们三年前 ＿＿＿＿＿＿＿＿＿＿＿＿ 。    a.開始談戀愛    b.談起戀愛來

2.他剛才很生氣，現在＿＿＿＿＿＿ 。    a.開始高興        b.高興起來了

3.今天我們十二點 ＿＿＿＿＿＿＿＿ 。    a.開始上課        b.上起課來

4.他走着走着，突然＿＿＿＿＿＿＿＿ 。    a.開始跑         b.跑起來

5.他以前是教中文的，怎麼現在＿＿＿＿？    a.開始教日文了    b.教起日文來了

6.他病得很厲害，不知道什麼時候才會＿＿＿＿ 。    a.開始好    b.好起來

# 閱讀練習

### 頭疼的結果

    雅克今天有個頭疼的問題[1]：他不想上課，想約女朋友出去玩。可是他的老師很嚴格[2]，說要有醫生證明才可以請假。怎麼辦呢？雅克想了一個辦法。他到醫務室去看病，跟醫生說他不但頭疼、肚子疼，而且還發燒了。醫生先給他量體溫，雅克趁醫生不注意的時候，趕快把溫度計[3]放進一杯熱水裡，然後又放進嘴裡去。過了一會兒，醫生看了看溫度計，差不多四十度！高燒[4]！再看看雅克的樣子，摸摸[5]他的頭，說，"奇怪！你的頭怎麼不燙啊？"雅克說："我也不知道怎麼搞的，可是我真的不舒服。哎喲，我的頭真疼！哎喲—哎喲—怎麼搞的？這麼疼！"醫生趕快又聽了聽雅克的心和肺[6]，覺得也沒什麼問題。最後醫生說："你的情況有點奇怪，我現在還檢查不出問題在哪兒。"雅克說："那沒關係，只要[7]給我開個證明，我休息兩天說不定就好了[8]。"醫生說："我看啊，你不但得休息，而且得住院[9]好好檢查一下。現在什麼地方你都不能去，就待在急診室[10]裡。護士[11]

過一會兒會來帶你去檢查。"雅克説："哎呀，不行不行！我這幾天有很多課，還有考試！"醫生説："身體[12]重要[13]還是上課重要？而且，如果你的病會傳染[14]，去上課更不好了。別着急，我會給你開一個證明。"雅克只好[15]待在急診室裡了。他想："真要命！本來爲了跟女朋友出去玩才裝[16]病的。結果現在不但不能出去玩，而且還得住院檢查！——現在我倒真想上課了！"

生詞表（查出或猜出空着的詞的意思）：

1. 頭疼的問題 _____
2. 嚴格[yángé] strict
3. 溫度計 _____
4. 高燒 _____
5. 摸 _____
6. 肺 [fèi] lung
7. 只要 [zhǐyào] as long as
8. 好了 _____

9. 住院 [zhùyuàn] be hospitalized
10. 急診室 [jízhěnshì] emergency room
11. 護士 [hùshi] nurse
12. 身體 _____
13. 重要 [zhòngyào] important
14. 傳染 [chuánrǎn] contageous
15. 只好 _____
16. 裝 [zhuāng] to pretend

回答問題：下面説的對不對？爲什麼？

1. 雅克今天頭疼、發燒，而且肚子也疼，所以去看病。
2. 醫生量了體溫以後，説雅克發高燒，所以要好好檢查檢查。
3. 雅克的頭疼得很厲害，要醫生給他開一個證明。
4. 醫生覺得雅克的問題很怪，得住院檢查才行。
5. 雅克不想住院，因爲他想上課、考試。
6. 醫生説雅克的病會傳染，所以不能去上課。
7. 雅克最後很高興，因爲醫生要給他開證明，他可以休息兩天了。

# 口語練習

## I.練習下面的詞彙 (Practice the following terms)：

喉嚨疼 [hóulong téng] have a sore throat

皮膚痒 [pífu yǎng] have itchy skin

過敏 [guòmǐn] have an allergy, be allergic

胃疼 [wèi téng] have a stomach ache

食物中毒 [shíwù zhòngdú] have a food poisoning

打針 [dǎzhēn] have/give an injection

照X光 [zhào āikesi guāng] take an X-Ray

量血壓 [liáng xuèyā] take/check blood-pressure

 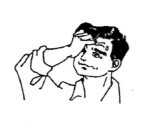  

## II.醫生在給病人做什麼？為什麼要這樣做？

## III.情景會話：看病

假設你病了，去找醫生看病。醫生（或護士）問你很多問題（有什麼感覺、哪裡不舒服、病以前吃過喝過什麼東西），然後給你檢查（量體溫、量血壓、聽心肺）。最後告訴你應該做什麼（吃藥、打針、休息、照X-光）。（請兩個同學一起練習。）

# 寫作練習

1.**看圖習作**：請把下圖的 "老李的假期" 寫出來。

請用下面的詞語：
真要命！　再......也沒有了！不知道怎麼搞的；早不...晚不...，偏偏在....
結果；不但...，而且...V着V着,...也...起來；越來越厲害；哎喲！怎麼這麼...

## 老李的假期

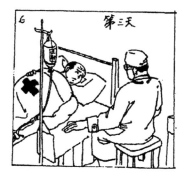

2.照下面的格式練習寫一張請假條(Follow the format below and write a note to your teacher asking to be excused from classes)：

## 請假條

王老師：

　　我這幾天感冒發燒，很不舒服。我剛看過病，醫生說我得休息兩天，所以今天明天我都不能來上課了，特此[1]向您請兩天假。（附上[2]醫生證明一份[3]。）

您的學生李大爲
九月二十日

Notes:

1. 特此 [tècǐ] (conventional use) "specially for this matter"

2. 附上 [fùshàng] (conventional use) "attached is..." "... attached"

3. 份 [fèn] (Measure word): [a] copy [of certifying letter, etc.]

# "海琳，我真想你！"
## —寫信—

第五課

語言情景　　語言結構　　文化介紹

Here, in Lesson Five, Dawei, far away from home in Beijing, pours out his heart in a letter to Hailin, who, you'll remember, is in Taiwan. So you'll learn a bit about letter writing in Chinese.

You will concentrate on one of the most prominent structural features of modern Mandarin: the Topic-Comment form of sentence.

You'll also learn about relevant culture and language when you write a private letter.

# "海琳，我真想你！"
## -- 寫信 --

親愛的海琳:

　　我真想你！你一定在等我的信吧？我到了北京以後，學校安排我們住在留學生宿舍樓裡。開始那幾天我很興奮，什麼對我都很新鮮。可是因為到了新地方，身體不適應，加上我又喜歡吃生冷的東西，結果生了一次病，在床上躺了兩天才好。還有就是不習慣這裡的上課時間：每天早上八點就得上課！我以前睡慣了懶覺，所以開始常常睡過了頭，第一個星期老遲到。老師對我們很關心、很熱情，可是也很嚴格。他們很重視學生的學習態度，説學得慢不要緊[i]，可是一定要努力。老遲到或者不上課他們就會認為是學習態度有問題。食堂的吃飯時間規定得也很嚴，去晚了就買不到飯了[ii]。好在這幾天我已經慢慢地適應這裡的生活了。

　　我住的宿舍是兩個人一個房間，我的同屋是一個名叫雅克的法國留學生。雅克是一個很有意思的人，跟我的性情很不一樣，習慣也不同。比方説，我晚上想安安靜靜地看看書、複習複習功課，可是他偏偏要在宿舍裡跟女生聊天，我只好去圖書館。有時候，他一邊聽流行歌曲，一邊跟着

---

i. 學得慢不要緊 ("It doesn't matter if one is slow to learn.") This type of structure in Chinese is normally referred to as the Topic-Comment Structure. See Structural Focus for more on this feature of Chinese. Note for now that in Chinese it is incorrect to reverse the word order by putting 不要緊 up front in the sentence as is often done in English.

ii.去晚了就買不到飯了 means "If you arrive late [then] you won't be able to get food". The pattern implies a sense of "if ... then...." 就 often signals this feature.

| 宿舍 | | sùshè | N dormitory, dorm-room |
|---|---|---|---|
| 加上 | | jiāshàng | MA/V plus the fact that. in addition; to add |
| -慣 | -惯 | guàn | RVE be accustomed to / be in the habit of ...; (吃慣了,睡慣了) |
| -過了頭 | -过了头 | -guòletóu | VP to overdo...; have overdone -睡過了頭 oversleep |
| 遲到 | 迟到 | chídào | V to arrive late (for class,meeting) |
| 熱情 | 热情 | rèqíng | ADJ warm-hearted, friendly |
| 嚴格 | 严格 | yángé | ADJ strict, harsh (can be shortened to 嚴) |
| 重視 | 重视 | zhòngshì | V to regard as important, take sth. seriously |
| 態度 | 态度 | tàidu | N attitude |
| 要緊 | 要紧 | yàojǐn | ADJ urgent, important |
| 努力 | | nǔlì | V to strive, work hard (to achieve sth.) |
| 認為 | 认为 | rènwéi | EV to think that..., believe that... |
| 食堂 | | shítáng | N cafeteria (of a school, hospital, etc.) |
| 規定 | 规定 | guīdìng | V/N to make it a rule that; rule, regulation |
| 好在 | | hǎozài | MA [colloq.] fortunately, luckily |
| 同屋 | | tóngwū | N room-mate (in Taiwan: 室友) |
| 性情 | | xìngqíng | N disposition |
| 比方說 | 比方说 | bǐfāngshuō | PH for example |
| 安靜 | 安静 | ānjìng | ADJ quiet (安安靜靜地,quietly) |
| 複習 | 复习 | fùxí | V/N to review (lessons); review |
| 功課 | 功课 | gōngkè | N course work, homework assignment |
| 聊天 | | liáotiān | VO to chat |
| 流行 | | liúxíng | ADJ popular (song, fashion, etc.) |
| 歌曲 | | gēqǔ | N song |
| 跟 | | gēn | V to follow |

錄音機大聲地唱，唱得我頭都大了。後來我想出<sup>iii</sup>了一個辦法，他一唱歌我就聽中文錄音，並且也跟着大聲地唸。這時候，他就會停下來<sup>iv</sup>聽我唸，然後説，“不對不對，你的四聲老錯。另外，唸書的時候要有感情，不要乾巴巴的<sup>v</sup>。聽我唸給你聽……”。雖然他也不見得比我唸得好，但總<sup>vi</sup>比他唱歌好聽多了。

在這裡還有好多事情我都不習慣，想吃的吃不着，想看的看不到。最難受的是親人朋友都離我那麼遠，有時候覺得真寂寞。所以我特別特別地想你，也常常想起我們在一起的時候很多有意思的事情。海琳，我得告訴你一件事：我發現我真的愛上你了，不然怎麼會這麼想你呢？有時候真是想得睡不着覺。你是不是也這麼想我？

你的情況怎麼樣？希望你一切<sup>vii</sup>順利。給你寫完這封信，我心裡舒服多了。希望儘快收到你的回信。真想現在就看見你！

祝

好！

想你的　　大爲

九月十五日，北京

---

iii. 想出來 ("to think up" "come up with") is different from 想起來 ("recall", "remembered [by recalling]") in that 想出來 suggests coming up with something original (e.g.,一個辦法："solution") while 想起來 implies recalling something already in one's memory (e.g.,他的名字）.

iv. 下來 is a resultative ending which can be added to a verb or adjective (stative verb) to indicate a transition from one state, physical or emotional, to another, e.g. from motion to stillness. For example,車停下來了 (The car came to a stop); 晚上十二點以後，外面才安靜下來 (Only after midnight did it finally begin to quiet down outside.)

v. 巴巴 here is an adjectival suffix used to add vividness to the word干 (dry). This kind of usage is very common with adjectives of state or appearance, such as 冷冰冰 (lěng bīngbīng: icy cold/coldly), 笑嘻嘻 (xiào xīxī: smilingly), etc.

vi. 總比他唱歌好聽多了 ("At least it was far more pleasant than his singing"). 總 here is an adverb implying "after all", "at least","in any case".

| 錄音機 | 录音机 | lùyīnjī | N tape recorder (錄音, V/N to make a tape recording; recording, tape) |
|--------|--------|---------|------|
| 並且 | 并且 | bìngqiě | MA moreover, and, and also (syn. ěrqiě, 而且) |
| 唸 | 念 | niàn | V to read aloud, chant (poem, etc.) |
| 停 | | tíng | V to stop |
| 感情 | | gǎnqíng | N emotion, feeling |
| 乾巴巴 | 干巴巴 | gānbābā | ADJ dry and dull |
| 不見得 | 不见得 | bújiànde | MA [colloq.] not necessarily |
| 寂寞 | | jìmò | ADJ lonely |
| 發現 | 发现 | fāxiàn | V/N to discover, find; discovery, finding |
| 愛上 | 爱上 | ài shàng | RV to fall in love with |
| (要)不然 | | (yào)bùrán | MA otherwise |
| 一切 | | yíqiè | N all; everything |
| 順利 | 顺利 | shùnlì | ADJ/A (progress of a matter) smooth; smoothly, without a hitch |
| 儘快 | 尽快 | jǐnkuài | A as soon as possible, soon |
| 收到 | | shōudào | RV to receive [mail, gift, etc.] |

判斷出以下詞語的意思：
睡懶覺　　　　睡懒觉
頭大　　　　　头大

vii. 一切 (everything, all), a pronoun or noun, behaves differently from 所有的... (all of the ...),which is used as an adjective to modify a following noun. 一切 is normally non-specific, whereas 所有的 usually has a specific reference.
Compare:
　　這裡的一切都很有意思。 Everything here is interesting.
　　一切都很順利。 Everything went very smoothly.
　　所有的書都很有意思。 All the books [you gave me, etc.] are interesting.
　　所有的問題都可以解決。 All of the problems [that we have, etc.] can be solved.

| 和平 |  | hépíng | ADJ/N peaceful; peace |
|------|------|--------|----------------------|
| 轉 | 转 | zhuǎn | V to foward, transfer; (envelope) care fo (c/o) |
| 地址 |  | dìzhǐ | N address |
| 信封 |  | xìnfēng | N envelope |

信封、地址

中國北京
北京大學留學生宿舍樓312號
李大爲

台北市和平東路三段五號二樓203室

吳興國　先生　轉
吳海琳　小姐　收

回答問題：
1.大爲對新的生活適應得怎麼樣？
2.大爲和同屋雅克有些什麼不一樣的地方？
3.大爲喜歡他的新環境和新生活嗎？爲什麼？

# 語言結構
## Focusing on Structure

## The Topic-Comment Structure in Chinese

It is often said that sentences in colloquial Chinese are to a great extent structured as Topic-Comment rather than the Subject-Verb formatting of English. What is a Topic? Basically, itüs what the sentence is about. A Topic-Comment sentence, to put it simply, consists of two major components: Topic and Comment. The Topic (which may range from a single word to a complete clause) almost always appears at the beginning of the sentence and orients the listener to what the coming message is to be about. The Comment supplies information about the Topic. The Topic can be longer or more complex than the Comment. For example, to express the idea "It is not good to watch TV while you eat," you may say "你一邊吃飯一邊看電視不好."Note the longer Topic and short Comment (不好). By the way, it is incorrect to reverse the order with something like: *不好你一邊吃飯一邊看電視.

What distinguishes Topic from Subject is that the subject always has a direct relationship with the verb but the Topic may or may not coincide with the subject since the Topic is determined by the context in which a given sentence occurs. In English, nearly all sentences must have a subject. Not so in Mandarin where the concept of Topic is much more significant.

Study the following examples and see if you can get a feeling for the Topic-Comment structure. The topic of each sentence is underlined.

那本書我已經看完了。 (Compare 我已經看完那本書了。)
　　(As for) That book, I have [already] finished reading it.
她英文不好，所以沒出國。
　　She was poor in English, so she didn't go abroad.
我頭疼，他肚子疼。( Note the two topics)
　　I have a headache, and/but he has a stomach ache.
這件衣服你穿很好看。 (Compare 你穿這件衣服很好看。)
　　This jacket looks good on you.
飯已經做好了。
　　The food is prepared/done now.
你的名字怎麼寫？(Don't say 你怎麼寫你的名字。)
　　How do you write your name?
那個學校學生多老師少。
　　In that school, there are many students but few teachers.
在中國學中文很有意思。
　　It is fun to study Chinese in China.
三天不吃飯没關係。
　　It doesn't matter if (you) don't eat for three days.

# 辭彙用法
## Word Usage

### Verbs
- 等：等人；等信；等電話；等車；等車等了半天；没等到人
- 躺：躺在牀上；在牀上躺着；在牀上躺了半天；躺得很舒服
- 遲到：上課遲到；開會遲到；遲到了半個鐘頭；常常遲到
- 重視：重視學習態度；對環境衛生很重視
- 認爲：他認爲你的中文很好。/你認爲他怎麼樣？/我認爲…；我不這麼認爲
- 規定：上課時間規定得很嚴格。/老師規定我們一天學一課。學校的規定；這
       裡的規定很嚴格。(N)
- 複習：複習功課；複習生字；複習課文；好好複習複習
- 停：把車停下來；你把車子停在哪裡？/不停地唱(説、吃、走) (Adv)
- 發現：發現新東西；發現了什麼？/在哪裡發現的？/新發現；有什麼發現？(N)
- 轉：轉信；轉車；轉學；把信轉給他；這封信轉了三次才到我這裡。
- 跟：跟着我走；跟着我説；别跟着録音機唱；你怎麼一天到晚老跟着他？

### Verb-Object Compounds/Phrases
- 聊天：跟朋友聊天；聊天聊得很高興；聊了三個鐘頭的天；没時間聊天

### Resultative Verb Compounds/Phrases
- V上：愛上；喜歡上；看上
  我想他愛上你了。/我喜歡上中文了。/
  我媽媽看上了那個人，想讓我跟他結婚，可是我看不上他。

- V慣：吃慣；喝慣；用慣；住慣；寫慣
  這個菜有一點辣(là:spicy)，你吃得慣吃不慣？
  我喝慣了茶，所以喝不慣冷水。/很多中國人喝不慣冷牛奶。
  我用慣了大電腦，用不慣這種小電腦。
  他住慣了安靜的地方，不想到北京去住。

### Adjectives
- 熱情：對人很熱情；熱情地招待客人；他是個很熱情的人。
- 嚴格：要求很嚴格；嚴格的老師；對學生很嚴格
- 安靜：安靜的地方；安安靜靜地看書；他很安靜；吃了藥，他總算安靜下來了。
- 順利：生活很順利；一切都很順利；祝你學業順利！順利畢業
- 要緊：要緊的時候；這件事很要緊。/這個問題很要緊。/考得好不好不要緊。

### Nouns
- 態度：學習態度；工作態度；對人的態度；他的態度很好。
- 辦法：好辦法；没什麼辦法；想辦法；想不出一個好辦法來
- 感情：唸書唸得很有感情；我跟他感情很好。/我對這裡没有什麼感情。

# 句型和習慣用語
## Sentence Patterns and Expressions

**1.** ......，加上......，結果...... ( ..., plus... then,[sth. happened])
- 他到了新地方，身體不適應，加上又喜歡吃生冷的東西，結果生了一次病。
  He had just come to a new place and wasn't accustomed to the new environment. More-over, he likes to eat raw or cold food; then, he got sick.
- 我沒做好準備，加上考試前又生了一次病，結果就考壞了。
- 甲：他怎麼又生病了？ 乙：他的身體本來就不好，＿＿＿＿＿＿＿
- He was not smart. Moreover, he was not diligent. As a result, he was not successful (順利) in doing anything.

**2.** 雖然......，但是總比......多了 ( Although...yet it's much more... than... )
- 雖然這個房子不夠大，可是總比宿舍好多了。
  Although this house is not big enough, it is much better than the dormitory.
- 雖然自己一個人住有一點寂寞，但總比跟別人一塊住舒服多了。
- 雖然他有一點自以為是，＿＿＿＿＿＿＿＿＿＿＿＿＿＿＿＿＿＿＿＿＿
- Although he has his problems, his life is still much easier (順利) than mine.

**3.** ......，好在...... ( ..., fortunately, ... )
- 我前幾天忙死了，好在他來了，幫了我不少忙。
- 我剛來這兒的時候，什麼都不習慣，好在現在已經慢慢適應了。
- 我本來不知道應該怎麼做，＿＿＿＿＿＿＿＿＿＿＿＿＿＿＿＿＿＿＿＿
- I couldn't speak a word of Chinese when I went to China last year. Fortunately, my friend came to pick me up as soon as I arrived at the Beijing Airport.

**4.** VP了 (+ comment) ( If/Once sb. [does/has done...], then [sth. will happen])
- 你得早一點到食堂去，去晚了就買不到飯了。
  You'd better go to the cafeteria earlier. If you go there late you won't be able to buy food.
- 你看電視的時候坐遠一點，坐近了對眼睛不好。
- 你放心吧，他吃了藥就會好了。

- You can go now if you have been excused from class by the teacher (請假).

## 5. (Clause) + （不要緊/很重要/很好/不好）(It is [unimportant / important / good/ bad,etc.] to/that...)

- 學得慢不要緊，可是一定要努力。
  It's OK if you are slow (in studying), but you must study hard.
- 醫生說，飯後休息一下再看書對身體很重要。另外，躺着看書也不好。
- _____,我們會等你的。
- It doesn't matter that you live far away if you have a car.

## 6. 一邊(primary action) ......，一邊(accompanying action) ......( Sb. does/did one thing while doing another )

- 他一邊看書，一邊聽 流行歌曲。 He listened to hit/popular songs while reading.
- 你不要一邊吃飯，一邊說話。
- 我喜歡 _____
- This year she is studying medicine in school and is working in the school clinic at the same time.

## 7. (Clause), V/Adj. 得 sb.(+ result/extent )(...so much so that it causes/caused...)

- 他老在宿舍裡唱歌，唱得我頭大。
  He always sings in the dorm and that drives me crazy.
- 他老看着我，看得我不好意思。
  He was always staring at me, which made me feel uneasy.
- 這個地方太安靜了，安靜得我 _____
- He kept talking about this, and that gave me a headache.

- We walked for over ten hours, which made us totally exhausted.

# 文化介紹

Learning About Culture

## 中國人寫信的稱呼方式及一般格式

**Some Conventions Used in Writing Letters in Chinese**

There are many things that the foreign learner of Chinese has to pay attention to when writing letters in Chinese. First of all, there's the question of how to address the receiver. This involves some degree of language and cultural sensitivity. 大爲 starts out with: 親愛的海琳 -- "Dear Helen/My dearest Helen." Use of 親愛的 implies a very close relationship so we can imagine that as soon as 海琳 read the salutation, she knew that this letter was going to contain some very personal remarks. '親愛的 - so and so', can be used in a letter, for example, when parents address their children, or children their parents, or a woman her close female friend (a man does not address another man by this term, no matter how close they are), or, in the case of our lesson text, when two people in love address each other.

As we have told you before, addressing a person in Chinese, whether face to face in a conversation or in a letter, is always a culturally sensitive area. For letters, and in conversations for that matter, it is normally best and advisable for foreigners to address the person by his or her surname with a title, (when the title is known). So it's Lǐ lǎoshi, (李老師：Teacher Lǐ), Lǐ yīshēng (李醫生：Doctor Lǐ) or Lǐ jīnglǐ (李經理：Manager Lǐ), etc. Until you get used to some of the conventions (see below for some of these), get the advice of your teacher or a Chinese friend for your first few attempts at letter writing. But do try! It's a great way to make friends!

Here are some useful words and phrases you might use when writing a letter:

稱呼 (chēnghu) (**Terms of address**):
• 尊敬的李先生：您好！(very respectful)
• 李先生\女士\太太\小姐：您好 (polite)
• 李老師（醫生，伯伯，etc.）您好 (to a teacher, doctor, senior, etc.)
• 親愛的海琳：你好！\我很想你！(to a family or intimate relationship!)
• 李大爲 (or:大爲)：你好！ (to a friend)

### 信的開頭 (the opening remarks)

- 你近來好嗎\怎麼樣？
- 好久没有給你寫信了。
- 你的來信上星期收到了。
- 最近一直很忙，所以到現在才給你回信。
- 收到\看了你的來信我很高興。

*(After the opening remark(s) the body of the letter follows)*

### 信的結尾 (xìn de jiéwěi) (the letter's end/concluding remarks, usually including best wishes for the other person's health, regards to family, etc.)

- 祝好！
- 祝（你）萬事如意/一切順利/愉快/身體健康/學習進步
- 祝你全家好

### 落款 (luòkuǎn)(Sender's identification + signature):

- 您的學生 (name) 敬上 (jìngshàng, offered with respect) (from a student to a teacher)
- 你的好友 (name) （上）
(to a friend)
- 想你的 (name)
(to a close or intimate friend)
- 愛你的/想你的 (name)
(to boyfriend/girlfriend, spouse, or family)

### 時間、地點 (Date and locale)
九月十五日，北京

### 信封寫法 (Envelope format):

The Chinese sequence is opposite to what you're used to. In the West, it's the individual first, so, first the name, then street address, city, state, etc. But in China, it's the larger unit first, and so, like for many things in Chinese, you proceed from the general to the specific: country, city, street name and then house number, room number, and lastly, addressee's name (marked by 收, shōu, to be received by). Please note the varying formats on the following page.

## Western format:

Mr. Guoming Zhang
Foreign Student Office
Beijing Language Institute
15 Xueyuan Road,
Haidian District,
Beijing 100083
China

## Chinese format:

中國 100083
北京海澱區學院路15號
北京語言學院 留學生辦公室
張國明先生　　　收

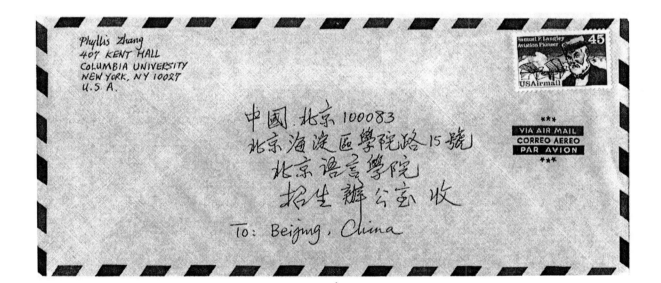

# 第五課聽力練習

## 第一部分：單句

請你們聽下面的句子。每個句子的意思是什麼？請在三個選擇中選出一句來。
Listen to the recorded statements.  Circle the sentence from the three choices which is closest in meaning to the statement heard.

1. (a)我吃得太飽了，沒力氣開車。
   (b)我開了長時間的車以後就沒力氣吃東西了。
   (c)我開了長時間的車，而且沒吃東西，所以特別累。

2. (a)我們找了半天，但是沒發現什麼。
   (b)我們找到了一封信，這是個很大的發現。
   (c)我們雖然沒什麼大的發現，但最少還找到了一封信。

3. (a)雨大得我沒法子回家。
   (b)因為雨停了，所以我才能回家。
   (c)我一回到家雨就停了。

4. (a)你們得早點兒來才見得到老王。
   (b)你們早來晚來都沒關係，老王會等你們的。
   (c)你們別來得太早，老王很晚才會來。

5. (a)對我來說，聰明和努力一樣重要。
   (b)我只喜歡又聰明又努力的人。
   (c)對我來說，一個努力的人比一個聰明的人更好。

6. (a)你不應該在做功課的時候看電視。
   (b)你應該看電視，才能把功課做好。
   (c)看電視對做功課很有幫助。

7. (a)他們昨天晚上在我房間裡聊天、做功課。
   (b)他們昨天晚上在我房間裡聊天，所以我做不了功課。
   (c)他們昨天晚上不做功課，所以到我房裡來聊天。

## 第二部分：短文

第一遍:請你們聽懂這篇短文的大意，然後回答問題。

First Listening: Listen to the recorded story. Try to get a general idea of what it is about. After you listen, answer the questions.

問題：1.這個人現在住在哪裡？

    a)學校的宿舍裡     b)朋友的家裡

    2.她有幾個同屋？

    a)四個       b)三個

第二遍:請你們讀下面的句子，然後把這篇短文一段一段地再聽一次。聽
   完每一段後，看看這些句子說得對不對。

Second Listening: Read the following statements. Then listen to the story paragraph by paragraph and pay attention to details. After you listen to each paragraph, decide whether the statements about it are true or false.

第一段：  _____1.除了說話的人以外，她的房間裡還有三個人。

     _____2.她的同屋們的性情和習慣都差不多。

第二段：  _____1.美靜長得不漂亮，但是人很安靜。

     _____2.美靜常常在房間裡大聲說話、唱歌，讓人睡不好覺。

     _____3.美靜最喜歡待在圖書館裡複習功課。

第三段：  _____1.小文是個熱情、有意思的人。

     _____2.小文沒有早睡早起的好習慣。

     _____3.小文上課從來不遲到。

第四段：  _____1.小安的功課比這房間裡的另外三個人都好。

     _____2.小安只睡覺不運動，所以常常生病。

     _____3.小安覺得運動沒有念書重要。

# 第五課 練習
## 辭彙；句型；語法

I.填入適當的詞語：

1.昨天我＿＿＿過了頭了，所以瀉肚子了。/今天我＿＿＿過了頭，一直睡到下午兩點鐘才起牀。

2.小王常常＿＿＿＿遲到，可是今天＿＿＿＿遲到。/他從來＿＿＿＿＿。

3.學校的規定＿＿＿＿＿。/學校規定學生＿＿＿＿＿＿＿。

4.你得努力＿＿＿＿才能畢業。/他這幾個星期學＿＿＿很努力，所以考試考＿＿＿很好。

5.聊了＿＿＿天；聊天聊＿＿＿＿＿，所以沒有時間複習功課。

6.我發現中文＿＿＿＿＿。/我認為這是一個很＿＿＿＿的發現。

7.我們＿＿＿＿＿的事很順利。/老張談戀愛談＿＿＿不太順利。

II.填入適當的形式：

(A)用關聯詞 (Use connectors):要不然；結果；這樣；另外；加上；好在

1.我忘了今天有一個考試，＿＿＿＿我昨天晚上把學過的課都複習了一遍。

2.昨天的水果不新鮮，＿＿＿＿你又吃得太多，所以今天瀉肚子了。

3.如果你今天有空，我們就一塊兒去吃飯，＿＿＿＿＿可以好好聊聊。

4.我昨天忙着複習功課，睡得太晚了，＿＿＿＿今天早上睡過了頭。

5.他一定又睡過了頭，＿＿＿＿＿他怎麼到現在還沒來？

(B)用動結式 (Use resultative verb endings):-出來；-起來；-慣；-上；-下來；-好

1.這個車有問題了，一開就停（不）＿＿＿＿＿＿。

2.那個東西到底是誰給你的？你想＿＿＿＿＿沒有？

3.我們兩個第一次見面就互相喜歡＿＿＿＿＿了。

4.我想來想去，就是想不＿＿＿＿＿買什麼給她。

5.以前我不喜歡流行歌曲，現在聽＿＿＿＿＿，也就覺得好聽了。

6.不知道怎麼搞的，我老開不＿＿＿＿＿你的車。

7.醫生說這種病因為沒有很好的藥，所以現在還醫不＿＿＿＿。

(C)用兼語式 (Use the V1給 person V2 form E.g.,我念給你聽 )

1.我男朋友喜歡吃我做的中國飯，我就每個星期都＿＿＿＿＿＿＿＿＿＿＿＿＿。

2.你這個字寫得不對，來，我＿＿＿＿＿＿＿＿＿＿＿＿＿。

3.我想看他的畫，所以他就把他所有的畫都＿＿＿＿＿＿＿＿＿＿＿＿＿。

4.你有什麼辦法？能不能＿＿＿＿＿＿＿＿＿＿＿＿？ (use the reduplicated form for V2)


(D)用 "一切" 或 "所有" (Use"一切"or"所有"):

1.你今天得把＿＿＿＿＿＿＿的生字都寫完。

2.我希望你＿＿＿＿＿＿＿＿＿順利。

3.我對這裡的＿＿＿＿＿＿＿＿＿都覺得新鮮。

4.他把這一課＿＿＿＿＿＿＿＿＿的練習都做完了。

5.＿＿＿＿＿＿＿的人都來了，我們就開始上課吧。

6.我們班＿＿＿＿＿＿＿＿的學生都喜歡吃中國菜。


III.話題—說明句練習 (Topic-Comment Structure Exercises):

(A)把劃綫部分變爲話題重組句子(Rewrite each sentence using the marked part as topic):

1.我很喜歡在圖書館複習功課。

2.他把我的車開走了。

3.醫生給我開了證明，可是我沒請假。

4.我已經吃過藥了。


(B)翻譯下面的句子 (Translate the following into idiomatic Chinese. Use Topic-Comment structure).
(The topic of each sentence is underlined.)

1. It is important for a student to review after class the things he/she has learned.


2. It doesn't make any difference to me whether you care about her or not.


3. Excuse me, how do you get to the airport?


4. (As for) That place, I think it's better that you don't go.

# 閱讀練習

　　大爲在課後打網球的時候認識了一個叫王苹的女學生。大爲正好想找個中國學生練習口語，王苹也正好想找個美國學生練習英語，所以他們就約好時間交換語言，互相幫助。王苹叫大爲"李大爲"或者"大爲"，大爲叫王苹"苹"。可是大爲奇怪的是，怎麼每一次他叫"苹"的時候，王苹都有一點不自然。後來王苹告訴他，"你就叫我'王苹'或者'小王'吧。"可是大爲還是不習慣，總是叫王苹"苹"。有一次他說"苹，我想問問你，......"話還沒說完，不知怎麼搞的，王苹的臉一下就紅了，好像很不好意思的樣子。過了一會兒，王苹突然又笑起來，說"大爲，你是想問我問題對不對？所以你應該說'問'，第四聲，如果說成第三聲，就是'吻'，意思是——是——那個——就是你們說的'kiss'的意思。"大爲聽了，才明白爲什麼剛才王苹會不好意思，他也跟王苹一起大笑起來。

　　大爲進步得很快，慢慢地跟王苹也越來越熟了。有一天，大爲有一點急事，不能在約好的時間去跟王苹見面，所以他就急急忙忙寫了一個條子給王苹，上面說：

　　親愛的苹，

　　　　對不起，我今天有一點急事，要出去一下，可能七點鐘回不來跟你練習。那我們就下次在老地方見面好了。

你的　大爲

　　王苹看到大爲的條子上寫的是"親愛的苹"，而且下面還有"你的大爲"，嚇了一跳。想來想去，都覺得大爲並不像對她有特別的意思。對了，大爲一定用的是英文的寫法"Dear..." "Yours"。王苹想着想着笑起來了，也給大爲留了一個條。

　　大爲：

　　　　你給我留的條我看到了，你差一點要鬧個笑話！猜猜看是爲什麼。明天我們見面時我再告訴你。

你的朋友　王苹

**回答問題：下面説的對不對？什麼地方不對？**

1.大爲和王苹是別人介紹認識的。

2.大爲叫人的時候不習慣連姓一起叫，所以叫不慣"王苹"。

3.王苹聽不慣大爲叫她"苹"，因爲中國人從來不這樣叫人。

4.大爲鬧的笑話都是因爲對中國文化不太熟悉。

5.王苹聽不懂大爲的英語，常常自作多情，大驚小怪。

6.大爲的條子好像是寫給一個跟自己談戀愛的女朋友的。

7.王苹覺得大爲可能對自己有意思，所以也給大爲留了個條。

# 口語練習

I. 說明下面的詞的意思：（請舉例子）

他對人很**熱情**。/他工作很**努力**。/他很**寂寞**。/他生活很**順利**。

II. **敘述練習**：請看下面的圖，說一說馬克剛到北京的時候和後來的情況。

馬克在北京

## 有用的詞彙

1. 發音 [fāyīn] pronunciation

2. 聲調 [shēngdiào] tones

3. 不準 [bùzhǔn] inaccurate

4. 鬧笑話 [nào xiàohuà] to make a fool of oneself

5. 比方說 [bǐfang shuō] for example

6. 把A說成B　said B instead of A by mistake

7. 吻 [wěn] to kiss

8. 把老師嚇一跳 [xià yí tiào] ...startled the teacher

9. 說夢話　to talk in a dream

10. 有很大進步 has made great progress

11. 流利 [liúlì] fluent

12. 誇 [kuā] to praise

# 寫作練習

1.<u>給人留條子</u>

　　你原來跟老師約好今天來問問題或者談一點事，可是你正好有一點別的事情不能來了，所以你給老師留一個條子，想換一個時間。請照下面的格式寫：

_____老師：

　　我原來跟您約好_____來您辦公室_____，可是後來發現我今天正好_____，所以不能來了。我們能不能換一個時間？_____您有沒有空？如果可以的話，請給我留個條或者打電話告訴我。我的電話是_____。謝謝！

您的學生_____上
____年____月____日

2.<u>寫一封申請留學的信</u>

　　你想到中國去留學，所以要寫一封申請信給中國的學校。信裡，先介紹你自己現在在做什麼，然後說一下你寫這封信是想申請留學。最後希望學校給你寄申請表和學校的情況介紹。請注意不要隨便用 "親愛的" "你的" 等等。（照下面的格式寫）

_____大學留學生辦公室：

　　我叫_____，中文名叫_____，現在是_____大學___年級的學生。我的主修是_____，並且學了_____年的中文。因為我_____，所以很想到中國來學習漢語。（除了_____以外，我也想學_____和_____。）希望你們給我寄一份申請表和其他有關材料[cáiliào: materials]。謝謝！

（你的中英文姓名）
____年____月____日

**從外國寄到中國的信封寫法**

(Return Address)

中國 (zip code)

(City name. street name and building number. room number)

(Name of office --if any)

(Name of recipient) (space) 收

**To: China**

**中國國內的信封寫法**

(Recipient's zip code in the boxes)

(City name. street name and building number. room number)

(Name of company or office )

(Name of recipient) (space) 收

(Return address: city. street name and number, room number. surname)

(Sender's zip code -->)

## 3.寫中文信封

請按中文格式寫兩個信封，一個是國際信封，一個是中國國內的信封。

A.國際信封：

寄信人姓名、地址：（寫你現在的英文地址、姓名）
收信人姓名：　　　招生辦公室
地址：　　　　　　中國北京海澱區學院路15號
　　　　　　　　　北京語言文化大學
郵編：　　　　　　100083

**從外國寄到中國的信封寫法**

To: China

B.中國國內信封：

　　　　收信人姓名：　　劉中華
　　　　　　地址：　　　昆明環城南路218號
　　　　　　　　　　　　昆明中國國際旅行社
　　　　　　郵編：　　　650011
　　　　寄信人姓名：　　（你的名字，用英文和中文）
　　　　　　地址：　　　北京海澱區學院路15號
　　　　　　　　　　　　北京語言文化大學留學生宿舍10號樓213室
　　　　　　　　　　　　郵編：100083

中國國內信封寫法

# "喂，麻煩你找一下李大爲"
## ─打電話─

第六課

語言情景　　語言結構　　文化介紹

This lesson finds Hailin in Taipei, anxious to make contact with Dawei.

In the process, you will learn some useful things about making a telephone call using Chinese.

As far as grammar is concerned, you'll look at creating emphasis and expressing feeling with the adverbial intensifiers, 真，好 and 多麼。

Culturally, you'll find out about the language and cultural conventions used when Chinese make a telephone call.
(中國人打電話的語言格式)

# "喂，麻煩你找一下李大爲"
## --打電話--

　　自從海琳到了台北以後，就盼望着大爲來信，特別是伯母跟她說了要給她介紹對象的事以後，她就更着急了。可是左盼右盼[i]都不見大爲的信來，數一數已經過了兩個星期了。海琳想，一定是大爲已經把她忘了。想到這裡，她很傷心。她對自己說，算了，自己也忘了他吧。可是越說忘越忘不了[ii]，一閉上眼睛就想起大爲來。這一天，趁伯母不在家，她決定給大爲打一個電話試試看。大爲的電話眞不好打，不是佔線，就是沒人接。撥來撥去，最後總算接通了大爲的宿舍樓。

（叮———）

接線員：你好。要哪裡？

海琳：喂，這是從台灣打來的長途。我想找一下漢語中心的美國留學生李大爲。 麻煩你轉一下。

接線員：他住哪一個房間？你有他的分機號碼嗎？

海琳：沒有。能不能請你幫我查一下？他是今年剛去的。

接線員：請稍等。......我查到了，他住312房間，分機號碼是8061。我給你轉過去。

海琳：麻煩你了。

接線員：沒事。.....對不起，小姐，沒人接，你等一會兒再打吧。

海琳：那我能不能留個話？喂——喂喂——......怎麼搞的？人家[iii]話還沒說完她就把電話掛上了，眞氣人！

---

i. "左盼右盼", zuǒ pàn yòu pàn, ("keep longing for... "). This construction is similar to the Ｖ來Ｖ去 (看來看去) construction, because both refer to doing something "over and over again.ã The difference between 左Ｖ右Ｖ and Ｖ來Ｖ去 lies in that the 左/右 construction is not normally used with movement verbs while the 來/去 form is far more flexible and more often used with verbs implying movement.
Compare:
　　我左想右想，還是想不出一個辦法來。（=想來想去）
　　他在那裡走來走去/跑來跑去。（ Not! 左走右走 or 左跑右跑 ）
ii. "她越想忘越忘不了." ("The more she wanted to forget [him] the less she was able to"). 越 ... 越 ... = " the more ... the more ... ." Here are a couple of examples using 越 [positive]...越 [negative] construction:
　　你越想知道我越不想告訴你。 The more you want to know the less I want to tell you.
　　我越想睡着就越睡不着。The more I want to sleep the less I am able to.
iii. 人家 ("other person") is an indirect way to refer to oneself. It can also be used to refer to a third party understood, as in:
　　你現在就去啊？人家可能還沒回來呢。"Are you going now? They're probably not back yet."

| 喂 | | wéi/wèi | INTERJ Hello! (mostly used on the phone) |
|---|---|---|---|
| 自從 | 自从 | zìcóng | MA (ever) since |
| 盼望 | | pànwàng | V/N to look forward to; expectation |
| 着急 | | zhāojí | V/ADJ to worry; be worried |
| 數 | 数 | shǔ | V to count (numbers etc.) |
| 傷心 | 伤心 | shāng//xīn | VO/ADJ to hurt feelings; sad, heartbroken |
| 算了 | | suànle | IE "Forget it." "Never mind." |
| 閉(上) | 闭(上) | bì(shang) | RV to close (eyes, mouth, etc.) |
| 趁 | | chèn | CV take advantage of (a favorable situation) |
| 佔線 | 占线 | zhàn//xiàn | VO [of phone line] be busy, occupied |
| 撥 | 拨 | bō | V to dial (the telephone), set/adjust (a watch, dial, etc.) |
| 接 | | jiē | V to connect; to answer (phone) |
| 通 | | tōng | V get through (on telephone) |
| 按 | | àn | V to press; push down, depress |
| 叮 | | dīng | (sound simulation of a phone ring/bell) |
| 接線員 | 接线员 | jiēxiànyuán | N (phone) operator |
| 長途 | 长途 | chángtú | N long distance; long distance phone call |
| 分機 | 分机 | fēnjī | N (of phone system) extension |
| 號碼 | 号码 | hàomǎ | N number (room, phone,etc.); code |
| 查 | | chá | V to check, check over; look up (name, phone number, etc.) |
| 稍等 | | shāoděng | PH "One moment,please" "I'll be with you shortly", "Hold on" |
| 留 | | liú | V to leave (sth. for sb.) |
| 留話 | 留话 | liú//huà | VP to leave a (verbal) message |
| 人家 | | rénjiā | N [colloq.] the other person, other people; a 3rd person or the speaker himself/herself) |
| 掛 | 挂 | guà | V. hang; hang up (a phone); to ring off (sb. on the phone) |
| 小時 | 小时 | xiǎoshí | N. hour (syn. of 鐘頭) |

（兩個小時後。海琳再次撥電話。叮———）

——：（錄音）你好。請按對方的分機號碼。
（海琳按分機號碼。......嘟—嘟—）

——：喂？

海琳：喂，麻煩你找美國留學生李大爲接一
下電話好嗎？

——：好，你等一下。......大爲，你的電話！
是個女的，快一點！

大爲：喂？

海琳：喂，是大爲嗎？

大爲：我就是[iv]。請問是哪一位？

海琳：大爲，是我！你連我的聲音都
聽不出來了嗎？

大爲：是你—海琳！真沒想到你會打
電話來！我給你的信這麼快就到了？

海琳：你的信？你給我寫信了嗎？

大爲：寫了。你還沒收到嗎？信真慢！
海琳，我很想你，我真高興你來電
話！你怎麼樣？還好嗎？

海琳：還可以。大爲，有一件事我不知道
該怎麼辦，你給我出出主意。

大爲：什麼事？

海琳：伯母要給我介紹對象！

大爲：對象？對象是什麼？

海琳：哎呀，這你都不知道啊？就是——男朋友！不過，不是一般的男朋
友，是要結婚的那種男朋友。伯母說過幾天就帶我去見他。

大爲：真的？......那你——去嗎？

海琳：你說呢？

---

iv. "我就是。" （"This is he/she speaking"）Note the difference between Chinese and English formu-
laic telephone expressions. See the 文化介紹 for more on this.

大爲：當然不去。

海琳：你是說你不願意我去跟他見面？

大爲：對，我是ˇ不願意你去。海琳，我真的愛你。你不知道我多麼想你！
如果你也愛我，那就跟你伯母說，你已經有男朋友了，不必找什麼
藉口。

海琳：其實我已經跟我伯母說過你是我的男朋友了，可是她說我是自作多
情。還說要我趁早跟你一刀兩斷呢。……大爲，我好想你啊！

大爲：我也很想你。真希望你現在也在北京！對了，你的電話號碼是
多少？……你說什麼？我聽不清楚，你大聲一點。怎麼有一個怪
聲音？海琳——喂——

海琳：喂——喂——怎麼搞的？怎麼沒聲音了？大爲！——

大爲：喂喂喂——這個該死的電話！偏偏在要緊的時候斷了。咳(H i)！

| 對方 | 对方 | duìfāng | N the other party |
| 嘟 | | dū | (sound of tone heard on the phone) |
| 麻煩 | 麻烦 | máfan | V/N/SV to trouble; (put sb. to some) trouble; annoyance; troublesome |
| 出 | | chū | V to contribute, chip in (idea, money, etc.) |
| 主意 | | zhúyì | N [colloq] idea |
| 一般 | | yìbān | ADJ general, average, run of the mill |
| 趁早 | | chènzǎo | A (do) while you can (see *Patterns*) |
| 藉口 | 借口 | jièkǒu | N an excuse, a pretext |
| 其實 | 其实 | qíshí | MA actually, as a matter of fact |
| 好... | | hǎo... | A [for emphasis] so..., terribly, awfully (see *Focusing on Structure*) |
| 該死 | 该死 | gāisǐ | IE [colloq.] damn (lit. "deserve death") |

---

v. 是here marks stress. 是 can be inserted in almost any statement to add a confirming tone to something that
the speaker and listener are sharing. Note the difference in emphasis:
我想出國。I plan/want to go abroad. (simple statement of fact)
我是想出國，可是現在沒有機會。It is true that I want to go abroad but there's no chance now.
我沒學過中文。I haven't studied Chinese.
我是沒學過中文，可是很想學。It's true that I have not studied Chinese before but I would sure like to.

判斷出以下詞語的意思：

氣人　　　　　　气人
出主意

回答問題：

1.為什麼海琳想給大為打電話？她打得順利嗎？
2.大為給海琳出了什麼主意？你覺得他的主意怎
麼樣？

# 語言結構
## Focusing on Structure

"真"、"好"、"多麼"

"zhēn," "hǎo," **and** "duóme" **as Intensifiers**

真，好，and 多麼 are often used before an adjective/stative verb or a verb in colloquial Chinese to achieve emphasis. The various tones achieved with such usages as well as the language situations appropriate for these "tonal adverbs" differ subtly, as illustrated below:

1. 真 expresses the speaker's heart-felt feelings, genuineness of sentiment, rather than the degree of feeling. It is mostly used in **dialogues** or **monologues** (i.e. mostly from the speaker's perspective).

**Examples:**

海琳，我真想你！Helen, I miss you so!

我真想現在就看見你！I wish I could see you right now!

我真高興你來電話！I'm (so) glad that you called!

信真慢！The mail is (so) slow!

(Note: These sentences do not sound natural without 真 or another adverb.)

**CAUTION:**

A. 真 sentences are not normally used in a narrative or descriptive manner. Nor should it be used when the speech is non-emotive. Here is an example of inappropriate usage:

*我住在一間真大的房子裡（correction:很大，好大，非常大）

*他去年開始學中文，他真喜歡中文（correction:很喜歡）

B. 真 is different from 真的 in that the latter means "really ... (as you/we have said)." 真的 is more confirmatory rather than emotion-laded like 真. Sometimes 的 is omitted and the learner has to judge which word is applicable from the context.

**Compare:** 他真壞！Oh he is bad!/He's the worst!

他真的很壞。He really is bad./He is truly bad (as we have said/have heard, etc.)

2. 好 is used often in speech as a modifier before an adjective/stative verb, a modal verb or even a noun. It intensifies the degree of the word it modifies, roughly corresponding to "badly", "terribly", "really", "awfully," etc. 好 can be used in conversational or descriptive contexts.

**Examples:**

大爲，我好想你啊！David, I miss you so much/a lot. / I really miss you.

她的眼睛好大！Her eyes are very big. / Her eyes are so big.

他買了一所好漂亮的房子。He bought a bea-u-ti-ful house.

哇！好一個聰明的孩子！Wow! What a smart kid!

3. 多(麼), is mostly used as a question word, e.g. 他有多（麼）高？It is also used sometimes with adjectives or modal verbs to express emphasis or exclamation. 不管我多（麼）忙，我也要去. However, this usage is only used conversationally. Notice in these examples how an exaggerated effect is achieved with 多麼. When it is used to intensify one's tone, the sentence often starts with such phrases as "你不知道..." or "看，...".

**Examples:**

你不知道我多（麼）想你！You have no idea how much I miss you!

看，這所房子多（麼）大！多（麼）漂亮！Take a look. How big and how beautiful this house is! (Look! Isn't this house big and beautiful!)

# 辭彙用法
## Word Usage

## Verbs

- 盼望：盼望朋友來信；盼望着家人來電話；盼望了很久才盼到
- 數：數一數有多少錢（人、字...）；數來數去；數了好幾次；數錯了
- 閉：閉上眼睛（嘴巴）；他的眼睛閉着。/他閉着眼睛想事情。
- 撥：撥電話；撥來撥去；撥了幾次；撥錯了號碼
- 留：留話；留字條；我給他留了一封信。/這個菜是留給你(吃)的。
- 掛：把電話掛上；電話掛斷了；給他掛個電話 (phone him)。/把畫掛起來，掛在牆上。
- 出：出錢(主意)；出了三千塊錢；出了一個好主意
- 麻煩：麻煩你幫我把那本書拿過來。/麻煩你幫我接一下電話。/這件事很麻煩。(Adj.) 別找麻煩。(N)
- 來\去：來電話(信)；他一直沒給我來電話。/我昨天給他去了一封信。
- 通：電話通了沒有？/這條路不通。/我跟他常常通電話。(通信：write to each other)
- 查：查一個名字（電話號碼、地址）；查查看有沒有這個人。/查到了；查不到
- 按：按這個號碼；按三下；按錯了

## Resultative Verb Compounds/Phrases

- V通：接通、打通、走通 (to get through by...)；電話接通了。/他的電話總是打不通。/這條路走不通，我們走那條路吧。
- V出來：聽出來，看出來，檢查出來 (detect by [listening, observing, checking])
  我聽不出來這是誰的聲音，你聽得出來嗎？
  你看得出來看不出來我是哪國人？
  我老頭疼，可是醫生沒有檢查出來我的問題在哪裡。

## Adjectives

- 着急：他很着急。/着急得不得了；為兒女的婚事着急；這件事真讓人着急。
- 傷心：他很傷心。/別為這件事傷心。/你這樣做真讓人傷心。/他傷了我的心。(VO)
- 一般：一般的朋友；一般人；一般來說 (generally speaking)；他的想法很一般

## Nouns

- 藉口：找一個藉口去跟他見面。/這不是一個好藉口。/我沒什麼藉口。

**1.** 不是 **A**,就是 **B (It is either A or B; If it's not A, it must be B)**
- 大爲的電話真不好打,不是佔線,就是没人接。
- 他每天都很忙,不是上課,就是工作。
- 我畢業以後,＿＿＿＿＿＿＿＿＿＿＿＿＿＿＿＿＿
- I guess he must be either Chinese or Japanese.

**2.** 自從......**(point of time)**以後,就 ...... 了 **( Ever since...., .... )**
- 他自從結婚以後,就没再給我打過電話了。
  He hasn't called me since he got married.
- 他自從大學畢業以後,就到中國去了。
- 他自從生過那次病以後,身體就越來越不好了。
- 自從學了中文以後,我＿＿＿＿＿＿＿＿＿＿＿＿＿＿
- I have been going abroad every year since 1983.

**3.** 左 **V** 右 **V** ,都**(neg.)**....../總算 **(pos.)**......了 **(kept doing sth, but still.../and finally...)**
- 我左盼右盼都盼不來他的信。
  I kept hoping to get letters from him, but I just never got any.
- 我左等右等都等不到他的電話。/我左等右等,總算等到了他的電話了。
- 他左看右看,＿＿＿＿＿＿＿＿＿＿＿＿＿＿＿＿＿
- I thought about it over and over again, but I just couldn't recall what his name is.

**4.** 趁......**V (taking advantage of... to do... )**
- 趁我父母不在家,我趕快給他打了個電話。
  Taking advantage of my parents' not being home, I hurriedly gave him a call.
- 我想趁年輕多念一點書。

- 他趁我不注意的時候 _____
- I asked him to come visit us when he would be in America next year.

## 5. 等......再 V......( wait until ... and then... )
- 等我把功課複習完了再跟你出去看電影。
  After I finish reviewing my lessons, I'll go to the movies with you.
- 等你想清楚了再做決定吧。
- _____來看你。
- He wants to hunt for a job after he graduates.

## 6. 趁早 V (do sth. as early as possible / while one can / before it's too late)
- 如果你不愛他，就趁早跟他吹了吧。
  If you don't love him, why don't you break up with him before it's too late.
- 我們最好趁早把飯準備好, 客人馬上就來了。
- 他叫我趁早_____
- In my opinion (我看), if you don't make preparations for going abroad early enough, you'll end up being too busy when the time comes (到時候).

## 7. 麻煩你 V...　 /麻煩你 V......好嗎？(Please [do me a favor and].../ Could you please [do...]?)
- 麻煩你請他接一下電話好嗎？　Could you tell him to answer the phone please?
- 麻煩你轉告他一下我明天去辦公室找他。
  Please (do me a favor and) tell him that I'll see him in his office tomorrow.
- 今天不能去上課，麻煩你 _____
- Could you please connect me with the foreign students dormitory?

# 文化介紹
## Learning About Culture
## 中國人打電話的語言格式
### On the Phone

China has still a long way to go before becoming a culture where the telephone is so much a part of the daily life of practically everyone, as it is in many Western countries. But things are changing rapidly and the telephone system of China, like other technology, is undergoing a genuine and rapid overhaul. Service is increasingly more convenient and even card phones and cellular phones are becoming more widespread.

China remains a society where face-to-face encounters are far more important and have the greatest effect on behavior. In a society such as China's, where telephone use is less widespread, the phone may act as a filter between individuals, making contact less personal, more distant, and, therefore, less subject to the usual rules of propriety. Perhaps for this reason, foreigners in China tend to feel that when conversing with Chinese over the telephone, Chinese etiquette and politeness, so commonly seen in other, more personal interactions, is temporarily suspended. Foreigners often complain that the Chinese party on the telephone is often blunt, abrupt, sometimes even rude. (Remember how mad 海琳 became when the operator hung up on her!) That sort of behavior, however, while occasionally encountered, is not an indication that the Chinese person is being deliberately rude. Generally, Chinese on the telephone come straight to the point without the usual niceties, with little ceremony, few greetings and fewer compliments.

打電話

**The following are examples of some useful 'telephone talk':**
打電話常用語舉例：

◆ Making a call and trying to locate your party
　　打電話

- 喂，請問李老師在嗎？
- 喂，我想找一下李老師。
- 喂，麻煩你請李老師接一下電話。
- 我能不能給李老師留個話？
- 我是李大中，麻煩你請他給我回個電話。我的電話是897-4654，分機號碼5353.

◆ Receiving/answering a call
　　接電話

- 喂，請問你找誰？
- (Operator)你好，你要哪裡？
- 你好，這是華南進出口公司，請問你找誰？
- (personal) (喂，) 我就是李明,請問（你是）哪一位？
- 對不起，他現在不在。請你等一會兒再打來。
- 他出去了，你有甚麼事？

◆ Asking the operator to put a call through
　　請接綫員轉：

- 喂，麻煩你轉一下5353。
- 喂，我有一個號碼老打不通，請你幫我轉一下好嗎？

◆ Asking for a telephone number
　　問號碼

- 喂，請問北京大學留學生宿舍的電話號碼是多少？

**Note**: When phone numbers are referred to in mainland China, "1" is mostly pronounced "yāo" and "0" is often pronounced "dòng". For example, "wǔdòng sān yāo" (5031) is more commonly heard than "wǔ líng sān yī".

# 第六課聽力練習

## 第一部分：單句

請你們聽下面的句子。每個句子的意思是什麼？請在三個選擇中選出一句來。
Listen to the recorded statements. Circle the sentence from the three choices which is closest in meaning to the statement heard.

1.　(a)留學生的生活都過得很好。
　　(b)離親人朋友遠一點兒真好！
　　(c)留學生離親人朋友很遠，生活非常寂寞。

2.　(a)她去台灣以前就很喜歡中國菜。
　　(b)她去了台灣以後就開始喜歡中國菜了。
　　(c)她太喜歡中國菜了，所以決定到台灣去。

3.　(a)小王想了很久還是想不出好法子來。
　　(b)小王隨便想了一下，就想出好法子來了。
　　(c)小王想了半天才想出好法子來。

4.　(a)你為什麼一邊等車一邊看書呢？
　　(b)你為什麼不藉着等車的機會看書呢？
　　(c)你為什麼等車的時候才看書呢？

5.　(a)我們得趕快談這件事。
　　(b)他回來以後不想談這件事。
　　(c)他回來以前我們不必談這件事。

6.　(a)等到明年你再作安排吧。
　　(b)你什麼時候作安排都沒關係。
　　(c)你還是早一點兒作安排吧。

## 第二部分：對話

請你們聽下面這兩個對話。聽第一遍的時候，請注意每個對話的大意。第二遍的時候，請注意細節。聽完以後，請回答問題。

Listen to the recorded two dialogues. After each dialogue, you will be asked some questions. When you listen for the first time, try to get a general idea of what each dialogue is about; at the second time, pay attention to details. After you listen, circle the correct answer for each question.

<u>請回答問題（對話一）</u>：

1.林文心為什麼打電話給小平？
    a)她想請小平幫她跟老師請假
    b)她想知道前兩天的法文課教了些什麼

2.小平是林文心的什麼人？
    a)同屋               b)大學同學

3.林文心為什麼已經兩天沒上課了？
    a)因為她請病假       b)因為她有一點累，想待在家裡休息

4.接電話的是小平的姐姐。她掛上電話以前跟林文心說什麼？
    a)她要林文心晚一點兒再打電話來
    b)她要林文心有空到她家去玩

<u>請回答問題（對話二）</u>：

1.接電話的人是誰？
    a)林文心的母親          b)林文心

2.林文心為什麼覺得很着急？
    a)因為她又沒上課又沒複習功課   b)因為她第一次打電話沒找到小平

3.下個禮拜一的法文課要考什麼？
    a)第六課的語法         b)第六課的生字聽寫

4.聽了小平的話以後，林文心覺得怎麼樣？
    a)她想只要她自己努力學習，考試就沒什麼問題了
    b)她覺得更緊張了

# 第六課 練習

## 辭彙；句型；語法

I.**選擇適當的詞語：**

1.這封信我已經_____了很長時間了。（盼望；希望；左盼右盼）

2.不知道怎麼搞的，上課的時候他老_____着眼睛。（閉；關；閉上）

3.他要打長途電話到台灣去，可是撥了好幾次都沒_____。（通；接；掛）

4.上個星期他們給我_____過兩次電話。（來；去；掛上）

5.這件事情我真不知道怎麼辦，給我出一個____吧。（主意；想法；辦法）

6.中國人_____都很重視親戚關係。（一切；一般來說；所有）

7.小李特別喜歡小張，常常_____藉口給她打電話。（發現，找；趁）

8.他的病真讓我_____。（着急；關心；傷心）

II.**選擇最適當的詞：**

1.你_____不愛他嗎？（好；真（的）；多麼）

2.這就是你五年前畫的嗎？_____不錯！（真；好；多麼）

3.他長得_____高_____高，差不多有兩米！（真；好；多麼）

4.去年他們買了一所_____漂亮的房子。（真；真的；好；多麼）

5.你看，這個地方_____漂亮！（真的；多麼）

6.我這幾天不舒服，所以_____不想去上課。（真；　多麼）

7.外面的雨_____大，看樣子我們今天出不去了。（真的；好；多麼）

8.哇(wow)！_____大的雨！（真的；好；多麼）

III.**用所給的句型改寫句子：**

1.我想趁朋友回國帶一點東西給我家裡的人。（藉...機會）


2.這本書我看來看去還是看不懂。（左Ｖ右Ｖ都......）

3.從我去年跟他分別的那天起，我就沒有再見到他。（自從......,就......了）

4.他的電話真難打！我左打右打，好在最後打通了。（V來V去，總算......）

5.現在他不在，我們最好先別做決定。（等......再V......）

6.結婚是我自己的事，我想跟誰結婚就跟誰結婚！（不管......都可以）

7.我們得現在就給他打電話，過一會兒他就會走了。（趁早......，要不然......）

8.我每次看見她的時候，她總是在打電話，要不然就是在跟別人聊天。
(不是......就是......)

---

# 閱讀練習

### 電話讓我們近了，也讓我們遠了！

　　電話真是給人帶來了1好大的方便2！你看，有了電話，你不必出門就能辦3很多事。如果有一個傳呼機4或者大哥大5，那麼不管在哪裡你都可以跟家人和朋友通話6。而且現在的電話機越來越 "能幹" 了，你想知道什麼它就會告訴你什麼，你自己連口7都不用開，只要用手按按8電話上的鍵9就行了。可以說，人們的生活越來越離不開電話了。

　　可是電話是不是讓人們的關係更親近10了呢？不見得11！至少12人們見面的時間是越來越少了。在沒有電話以前，你會常常找機會跟朋友見面，大家在一塊兒面對面地喝茶談天，很開心13。如果朋友住得遠，那麼大家會常常通信14。信雖然慢，但是能讓人更深15地交流16思想17和感情。可是自從有了電話以後，撥一個號碼就可以跟朋友說話了，多麼方便！多麼省18時間！現在不但打電話很方便，而且寫信可以用傳真機19或者電子郵件20，快極了。所以何必21再跑來跑去地去看朋友呢？何必再像以前那樣寫信呢？

　　結果怎麼樣呢？人們越來越懶22，慢慢地都把自己關23在家裡了：跟朋友的見面少了，見面的時間也短了24。所以可以說，電話讓我們近了，也讓我們遠了。

生詞表（查出或猜出空着的詞的意思）：

1. 帶來_____
2. 方便_____
3. 辦_____
4. 傳呼機[chuánhū jī]beeper
5. 大哥大 cellular phone
6. 通話_____
7. 口_____
8. 按[àn] to press

9. 鍵[jiàn] key (on a pad)
10. 親近_____
11. 不見得_____
12. 至少 [zhìshǎo]at least
13. 開心_____
14. 通信_____
15. 深[shēn]deep, deeply
16. 交流 [jiāoliú] exchange

17. 思想 thoughts
18. 省 [shěng]to save
19. 傳眞機 fax machine
20. 電子郵件 [diànzǐ yóujiàn] e-mail
21. 何必 [hébì] why bother...
22. 懶 [lǎn]lazy
23. 關_____
24. 短_____

回答問題：

1.這篇短文的大意是什麼？（請用兩句話說）
2.哪些例子說電話給人們帶來了方便？
3.爲什麼說電話也讓我們遠了？
4.現在人們跟家人、朋友的交往(interaction)跟以前有什麼不同？
5.你同意不同意作者的看法？爲什麼？

---

# 口語練習

I.語氣練習：

A.用“是”字加強語氣：

1.　　a.聽說你想去中國留學。　　b.我___想去中國留學。
2.　　a.你眞的沒收到我的信？　　b.我___沒收到你的信。
3.　　a.我不相信她給我回過電話。b.她____給你回過兩次電話，我知道。

B.用“好”“眞”“多麼”加強語氣和感情：

1.　　a.你學了兩年中文了，去過中國嗎？
　　　b.沒有，我想到中國去看一看。（眞）

2. a.我常用電腦給朋友寫信，你呢？
   b.我也常用。<u>很快、很方便</u>。（真）

3. a.那個人就是你要給我介紹的對象嗎？
   b.對。你看，他<u>長得高，也很帥</u>。（多麼）

4. a.你覺得那個地方怎麼樣？喜歡嗎？
   b.不喜歡。<u>天熱，房子貴，人也不客氣</u>。（好）

II.<u>請兩人一組練習下面的電話常用語：</u>

| 打電話的人 | | 接電話的人 |
|---|---|---|
| 喂，請問大爲在嗎？/我想找<u>一下</u>大爲。 | ----> | 我就是，請問（您）<u>是哪一位</u>？ |
| 喂，麻煩你叫一下王先生好嗎？ | ----> | 好，請（您）<u>稍等一會兒</u>。 |
| 喂，我姓張，我想找一下劉老師。 | ----> | 她不在。請問<u>您有什麼事</u>？ |
| 我有點要緊的事，我能不能給她<u>留個話</u>？ | ----> | 好的。請問您是哪一位？ |
| <u>麻煩你轉告她一件事,</u>... | ----> | 好。她回來我會告訴她。 |
| 麻煩你請他儘快給我回電話。 | ----> | 請問您的電話號碼<u>是多少</u>？ |
| 麻煩你轉一下305號房間。 | ----> | 對不起，現在<u>佔線</u>，請你過一會再打來。 |

III.<u>中文應該怎麼說</u>？

May I speak to Lisa, please?

This is she speaking.

What is your phone number?

Whom am I speaking with, please?

IV.情景會話：打電話跟人約時間見面

　　　假設你想約一個中國朋友出去看電影，你怎麼跟他/她約？

V.敘述練習：　"你撥錯號碼了！"

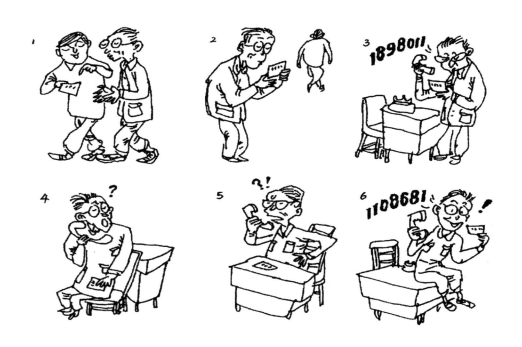

```
寫作練習
```

現在越來越多的人用電腦來做事情，比如說寫東西、通信、查資料等等。
請你談一下：

1.電子郵件跟電話、傳真機比，哪一個更方便？(請舉例)
2.用電子郵件有什麼好處和坏處？

有用的詞彙/句型：

| | | | |
|---|---|---|---|
| 雖然...但是 | 除了...以外 | 好在 | 其中 |
| 不但...而且 | 因為...所以 | 結果 | 認為 |
| 自從...以後 | 想(QW)...就(QW) | 另外 | 要不然 |

# "住在這裡再好不過了！"
## — 租房子 —

第七課

**Situation**     **Structure**     **Culture**

語言情景     語言結構     文化介紹

We're still with 海琳 in Taiwan, but you'll find her in this lesson striking out on her own: wanting to rent her own apartment. So she has a conversation with her landlord-to-be about room requirements and you'll learn a few things about a situation in which you may someday find yourself.

For Language Structure you'll look into the use of 使 in Chinese. In addition, you'll revisit the Presentative Structure (first introduced in Lesson Two), so take a look back to refresh yourself.

Culturally, since you are dealing with location structures, you'll learn a bit about traditional Chinese superstitions about locating a residence or business, in other words, the notion of fēngshuǐ. (中國人的 "風水" 觀念).

# "住在這裡再好不過了"
## --租房子--

　　海琳想自己租一間房子住，這幾天正在忙着找房子。她看到租屋廣告上有兩家房子對她比較合適，就給房東打電話約好去看房子。

　　第一家是一個兩房一廳的帶傢具的公寓，房子、地區都很不錯，可是海琳覺得那個房東要求太多，所以決定不要。她接着又去看第二家。

　　這一家也是一個兩房一廳的公寓。房東楊小姐看上去[i]很熱情。房間雖然沒有第一家那麼漂亮，可是也收拾得整整齊齊。客廳裡放着一套中式傢具，牆上掛着幾張中國畫，使人一進去就感到舒服。廚房、浴室也都打掃得很乾淨。更使海琳滿意的是，楊小姐沒有第一家房東那麼囉嗦。

海琳：楊小姐，我很喜歡你
　　　的這個公寓，可是不知
　　　道[ii]這裡的環境怎麼樣？
房東：我們這兒的環境很不
　　　錯，不但安全，而且坐
　　　車、買東西也都很方

---

i. 看上去（ "seem..." "look...") is close to "看樣子" in meaning. However, the former emphasizes physical appearance while the latter is used more figuratively ("seems like," "looks like..."). Compare:

　　他看上去不到三十歲。　　　　He looks under thirty.
　　看樣子他不到三十歲。　　　　He looks [like he's] under thirty./ He seems to be under thirty.
　　看樣子他不會來了。　　　　　It seems that he is not coming./ It looks like he is not coming.

Note also that when a noun phrase follows, 是(or 像 ) should be used. Compare:

　　他看上去很高興。　 He looks/looked happy.
　　他看上去是（ or像）一個大學生。　 He looks/looked like a college student.

ii. 不知道... is an idiomatic expression corresponding to "I wonder..." in English. Note that the word 我 is normally omitted since there is no other person assumed. The structure can be ended with a question mark if an answer is expected or a period if no answer is expected.

| | | | |
|---|---|---|---|
| 租 | | zū | V to rent |
| 廣告 | 广告 | guǎnggào | N advertisement |
| 房東 | 房东 | fángdōng | N landlord (of a rented house or building) |
| 廳 | 厅 | tīng | N hall, parlor |
| 客廳 | 客厅 | kètīng | N living-room, parlor |
| 傢具 | 家具 | jiājù | N furniture |
| 公寓 | | gōngyù | N apartment; apartment building |
| 地區 | 地区 | dìqū | PW area, region |
| 接着 | | jiēzhe | MA subsequently, then, immediately, next |
| 楊 | 杨 | Yáng | N (a Chinese surname) |
| 看上去 | | kànshàngqu | VP to look (young, tired, etc.) |
| 整齊 | 整齐 | zhěngqí | ADJ neat, orderly |
| 套 | | tào | M set of (furniture, books, etc.); suit (of clothing, etc.) |
| -式 | | -shì | BF -style |
| 中式 | | zhōngshì | MOD Chinese-styled (e.g., 中式傢具 ) |
| 廚房 | 厨房 | chúfáng | N kitchen |
| 浴室 | | yùshì | N bathroom (with or without toilet) |
| 打掃 | 打扫 | dǎsǎo | V. to clean (by mopping or sweeping) |
| 使 | | shǐ | V to make (sb/sth.)..., cause (sb. to VP) (syn. of 讓 ) |
| 滿意 | 满意 | mǎnyì | ADJ satisfied, content, happy with |
| 囉嗦 | 啰嗦 | luōsuo | ADJ [of a person] repetitious and fussy |
| 安全 | | ānquán | ADJ safe, secure |
| 往 | | wǎng | CV toward, to, in the direction of |

便。出了公寓樓往右拐，走到巷口就是一條大馬路，路的兩邊有很多商店，那裡可以說什麼都有。從巷口往左走幾步就是郵局和銀行，附近巷子裡還有幾家不錯的咖啡屋和小吃店。另外，這個公寓樓後面還有一個公園，我每天都去那裡運動。

海琳：住在這裡真是再好不過了！那[iii]請問你對房客有什麼特別的要求沒有？

房東：沒有什麼特別的要求，只要按時交房租，保持房間裡乾淨，另外注意安全就好了。對了，還有一點就是不可以吸煙。

海琳：這你放心。請問房租是多少？

房東：包括水電費在內，每月四千二。如果你決定要租了，得先給我定金。

海琳：你看這樣好不好：我先回去跟我的親戚商量一下，明天再給你回話，怎麼樣？

房東：好，我明天等你的回話。

海琳：謝謝！再見。

房東：再見。

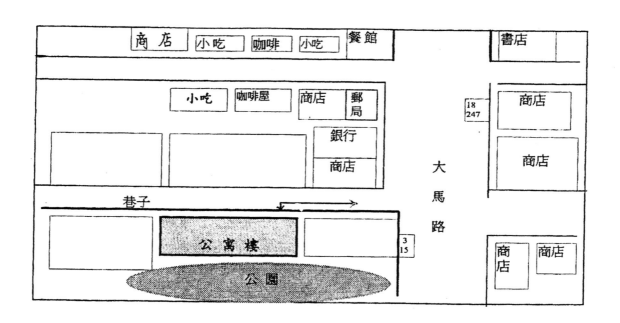

---

iii. 那 is used here as a sentence connective meaning "in that case" or "then."

| | | | |
|---|---|---|---|
| 拐 | | guǎi | V to make a turn (in direction) |
| 巷（子） | | xiàng(zi) | N alley, narrow street |
| 馬路 | 马路 | mǎlù | N boulevard, avenue |
| 商店 | | shāngdiàn | N store |
| 郵局 | 邮局 | yóujú | N post office |
| 銀行 | 银行 | yínháng | N bank |
| 公園 | 公园 | gōngyuán | N park |
| 房客 | | fángkè | N tenant |
| 只要 | | zhǐyào | MA as long as (often used with 就) |
| 按 | | àn | CV according to |
| 按時 | 按时 | ànshí | CV-O on time, [do...] according to scheduled time |
| 交 | | jiāo | V to submit, turn in; pay (rent, etc.) |
| 房租 | | fángzū | N rent (for a house or room) |
| 保持 | | bǎochí | V to keep (clean, etc.), to maintain |
| 吸煙 | 吸烟 | xīyān | VO to smoke (cigarette or cigar) |
| 包括 | | bāokuò | V to include, contain |
| 包括...在内 | | bāokuò...zài nèi | VP including, with.....included |
| 費 | 费 | fèi | N fee |
| 水電費 | 水电费 | shuǐdiànfèi | N utility cost ("water and electricity fee") |
| -金 | | -jīn | BF (lit. "gold") money, currency, a fund (used as N-Suf.) |
| 定金 | | dìngjīn | N deposit ( money paid in advance) |
| 商量 | | shāngliang | V to talk over (for a solution) |

判斷出以下詞語的意思：

| | |
|---|---|
| 兩房一廳 | 两房一厅 |
| 帶傢具 | 带家具 |
| 巷口 | 巷口 |
| 咖啡屋 | 咖啡屋 |
| 小吃 | 小吃 |
| 回話 | 回话 |

回答問題：
1.海琳是怎樣找房子的？
2.海琳覺得第一家怎麼樣？她爲什麼不要？
3.第二家跟第一家有什麼不同？爲什麼她喜歡第二家？
4.房東對她有什麼要求？
5.海琳最後的決定是什麼？你想她會不會租？
6.如果你找房子，你的要求是什麼？

# 語言結構
**F**ocusing on Structure

## I. Using "使" as a Causative Verb

使 denotes "making" or "causing" somebody to do something or enter (move, change) into a certain state. The subject or topic can be a person, a thing or an event (a noun phrase or a clause). A 使-clause can also be used as a topic (see Example C).

**Examples:**

    a. 今天的天氣使我（覺得）很不舒服。

        The weather today makes me uncomfortable.

    b. 這裡的生活條件真不好，使我很想回國去。

        The living conditions here are so poor that I want to go back to my country.

    c. 他看上去是中國人。可是，使我奇怪的是他一點中文都不會說。

        He looks Chinese. However, what surprises me is that he can't speak even a little bit of Chinese.

Note that 讓 and 叫 can be used the same way except that they sound casual.

## II. Location + 是 .. vs. Location + 有 ...

Both 是 and 有 are commonly used to introduce a place, a person, etc. into the discourse. However, they differ in meaning and structural requirements. 是 expresses that at a particular location, a person (object, place, etc.) is spotted or located while 有 indicates that something exists, among other things, at a particular location or place. The noun phrase after 是 can be either indefinite or definite; whereas with 有, the noun phrase is usually indefinite when it refers to a place.

    a. Location + 有 + indefinite noun phrase

        路的兩邊有很多商店。 There are many stores on both sides of the road.

        我們學校裡有三個圖書館。 There are three libraries in our school.

        *(學校對面有那家中國飯館　is incorrect because "那家" is not indefinite.)

    b. Location + 是 + (definite or indefinite) Noun Phrase

        那個大樓後面是一個公園。 Behind that building is a park.

        街對面是我們學校的圖書館。 Across the street is our school library.

# 辭彙用法
## Word Usage

## Verbs

- 租：租房子；租車；出租一個房間；我有一個公寓想出租。/ 你的房子租給誰了？/那個地區不好，房子租不出去。
- 打掃：打掃房間；你把房間打掃乾淨。/這幾個房間打掃得很乾淨。
- 保持：保持客廳的乾淨；保持水果的新鮮；保持好習慣；房間保持得很乾淨。
- 商量：商量事情；跟父母商量一下結婚的事；商量了半天；還沒商量好；有一件事我想跟你商量商量。/他們已經商量過了。
- 交：交錢(房租、學費、定金、功課)；把錢交給房東；功課明天交。

## Coverbs

- 往：往左走；往右拐；往前看；往後跑；往下跳
- 按時：按時上課(吃飯、睡覺、吃藥、做功課)；他常常不按時吃飯。

## Adjectives

- 整齊：房間收拾得整整齊齊的；他今天穿得很整齊。/麻煩你把書放整齊。
- 安全：這個地區很安全。/跟他在一起覺得很安全。/晚上出去要注意安全。(N)
- 滿意：對這個人(這件事、這個地方)很滿意；這個房子很讓人滿意。

## Nouns

- 廣告：租屋廣告；牆上貼着很多廣告。
- 地區：這個地區；北京地區；附近的地區；這個地區我不熟悉。/你住在哪個地區？

## Measure Words; Suffixes

- 套：一套傢具；一套住房；一套新衣服；一套書
- -式：中式傢具；西式廚房；美式英文(American English)
- -費：水電費；學費；車費；生活費；這裡的生活費很高。

## Other

- 接着：我先去買了點東西，接着我就去學校了。/他說，他已經找到了工作。他接着說，他很快就要去上班了。

# 句型和習慣用語
## Sentence Patterns and Expressions

**1. ...... 使 ......　(Sb. / Sth. makes / made sb. / sth. ....)**

* 他的話使我很高興。　His words made me happy./His words pleased me.
* 他學習不努力，使我很不滿意。

  He does not study hard and that makes me dissatisfied.
* 這裡什麼都好。更使我滿意的是，廚房又大又亮。
* 我的功課太多，使我 _____
* Removing these tables can make this classroom look larger.


**2. 忙着......( sb.is/was busy doing... [during/when...])**

* 這幾天她正在忙着找房子。　She is busy looking for a house these days.
* 他打電話來的時候，我們正忙着做飯。

  When he called us, we were busy cooking.
* _____ ，所以没時間給他回話。
* These days he is either busy making phone calls or visiting friends.


**3.看上去 ......(...looks/looked like...)**

* 她看上去只有五十多歲。　She looks like she is only in her fifties.
* 王老師看上去很嚴格。
* 甲：你覺得他怎麼樣？乙： _____
* She appears very smart and capable.


**4. 只要......（就）......(as long as..., then...; ... provided that...)**

* 只要你有錢，你就可以住很漂亮的房子。

  You can live in a beautiful house as long as you have money.
* 只要你不告訴他那件事，我就幫你的忙。

- 他說 _____ 不要緊，只要你喜歡他就行（了）。
- You can do whatever you want provided that you finish your homework first.


**5. 不知道......怎麼樣？( I wonder what...is like? )**

- 不知道這裡的環境怎麼樣？I wonder what the environment here is like.
- 聽說他的中文很好，不知道他的英文怎麼樣？
- 那個學校的規定很嚴格，_____
- I've never been to Taipei, and I wonder what the weather there is like.


**6. 包括......(在內)，......( Including..., ... [totals] ...; include .... )**

- 包括我在內，這裡一共有二十六個人。

  Including me, there are twenty-six people here .
- 不包括房租在內，你每個月要多少錢的生活費？
- 明天的考試包括這一課的生字（在內）。
- （不）包括 _____，我們學校_____
- Does your tuition cover fees for books?


- I have learned 500 new words so far, including this lesson's.


**7. (Location)就是 (Place)　　(Right at [location] is [place] / You'll find [place] right at [location] )**

- 出了大樓往右拐，走到巷底就是一條大馬路。Turn right after you get out of the building, walk to the end of the alley and (right there) you'll find a main street.
- 學校附近有一個中國飯館，對面就是他住的公寓大樓。There is a Chinese restaurant near the school. Right opposite it is the apartment building he lives in.
- 你一直往前走，_____就是東亞圖書館。

- Walk east after you get out of the school gate and right next to the Hong Kong Bank is the post office.

**Compare:** (place of concern) <u>就在</u> (location)

- 他住的公寓大樓就在中國飯館對面。

  His apartment building is right across the Chinese restaurant.

- 東亞圖書館就在_____。

- 我的宿舍樓就在_____。

Throughout the long history of China there has been a strong belief that all nature is made up of varying combinations of basic elements, and for things to be 'right' there must exist a harmony between such forces. This belief led in time to the development of a superstition that worked out just exactly how these forces or elements, five in number, metal, wood, water, fire and earth (金木水火土), should balance one another. (The parallel to the four elements of the Greeks [earth, fire, air and water] is striking.) Applied to the lay of the land--hills, mountains, valleys, bodies of water, manmade structures and so on --- the belief maintained that the positive and negative effects of physical things affected one's own fortune, one's good or bad luck. This belief led the Chinese to develop detailed guidelines for the location of houses, graves, business sites and even the layout of agricultural fields. This notion became geomancy (fēng-shuǐ, 風水 ), the influence of the 'winds and the waters,' i.e. the natural environment, on the life and luck of the individual.

Belief in the power of 風水 to play a role in the affairs of people is still very powerful in rural areas of China and also among Chinese in areas outside of China. Even today in sophisticated Hong Kong a geomancer (風水先生) is often consulted to review the plans of the architect before construction is begun.

The geomancer might recommend re-orienting a doorway (always a key point) to prevent the intrusion of baleful influences, or might suggest even more drastic redesigning, for the future health and happiness of the inhabitants will depend on the proper 風水 being implemented. If things are done in accordance with the principles of 風水 , prosperity results; if not, misfortune will ensue for sure.

# 第七課聽力練習

## 第一部分：單句

請你們聽下面的句子。每個句子的意思是什麼？請在三個選擇中選出一句來。

Listen to the recorded statements. Circle the sentence from the three choices which is closest in meaning to the statement heard.

1. (a)大房子住起來才舒服。
   (b)乾淨的房子使人住得舒服。
   (c)保持房子的乾淨不是什麼要緊的事。

2. (a)最近幾天學生們都在作考試準備。
   (b)考完試了，學生們現在都不忙。
   (c)學生們考試前一天才開始看書。

3. (a)看樣子這不是個好地區。
   (b)這個地區使人覺得不舒服。
   (c)這個地區看起來很不錯。

4. (a)我對他的工作態度很滿意。
   (b)我不喜歡他的工作態度。
   (c)我很高興跟他一起工作。

5. (a)我想知道她先生是什麼樣的人。
   (b)我對她先生很熟悉。
   (c)她先生人怎麼樣不重要。

6. (a)他只會說中文。
   (b)除了中文以外，他還會說兩種外國話。
   (c)他不懂中文，但是會說很多外國話。

# 第二部分：對話

第一遍：下面是小王和小林的對話。請你們聽懂這個對話的大意，然後看看下面這兩個句子說得對不對。

First Listening: Listen to the recorded dialogue between Xiao Wang and Xiao Lin. Try to get a general idea of what it is about. After you listen, decide whether these statements are true or false.

_____ 1.小林找來找去，忙了半天，可是還沒找到一個滿意的公寓。

_____ 2.小林的朋友小王想把他的房子租出去。

第二遍：請你們讀下面的句子，然後把這個對話再聽一次。聽完後，看看這些句子說得對不對。

Second Listening: Read the following statements. Then listen to the dialogue again. After you listen, decide whether the statements are true or false.

_____ 1.小林對他看過的幾家公寓都很滿意。

_____ 2.小林不喜歡住得離學校太遠。

_____ 3.小王的親戚正好有個公寓想出租。

_____ 4.小王想馬上帶小林去看他親戚的公寓。

第三遍：請你們讀下面的句子，然後聽第三遍。聽完後，看看這些句子說得得對不對。

Third Listening: Read the following statements. Then listen to the dialogue a third time and pay attention to details. After you listen, decide whether the statements are true or false.

_____ 1.小林看過的每一個房子都沒有帶傢具。

_____ 2.小林希望找一個帶傢具、房租便宜、環境安全，而且離學校不遠的公寓。

_____ 3.小王的親戚要到台灣去，半年後才會回來。

_____ 4.小王親戚的公寓附近沒有車站。

_____ 5.小王親戚的公寓房租不貴，而且還包括水電費。

_____ 6.小王想先問清楚房租是多少，然後再帶小林去看房子。

# 第七課 練習
## 辭彙；句型；語法

I.選擇填空：

1.我想在這個＿＿＿＿＿租一間房子。（地區；環境；部）

2.我有一間房子要＿＿＿＿＿＿。（租一下；租得出去；出租）

3.我把這間房子＿＿＿＿＿別人了。（出租；租出去；租給）

4.我＿＿＿＿這套房間很＿＿＿＿。（跟/舒服；對/高興；對/滿意）

5.這件事我得＿＿＿＿＿家裡商量商量。（跟；對；給）

6.你應該＿＿＿＿＿房間的乾淨。（整齊；保持；打掃）

7.他從來不＿＿＿＿交房租。（按時；按；保持）

8.客廳沒有打掃＿＿＿＿。（整齊；乾淨；收拾）

II.用所給的句型改寫下面的句子：

1.聽說北京大學很有名，我很想知道那裡的學費貴不貴。（不知道......）

2.我今年要去的地方有英國、法國、日本。（包括）

3.我住的那個地方不太好，郵局、銀行都很遠，我也不滿意那裡的飯館。
（......使我......）

4.看她的樣子是東方人。（......看上去......）

5.我現在一共學五門課，其中有中文課。（包括......在內,......）

6.那個大樓旁邊是東亞圖書館。（......就在......）

III.用 "使" 字結構改寫下面的句子：

1.我聽了他的話以後很滿意。



2.我從這本書裡學到了很多東西。



3.人吃了這種藥會興奮。



4.她說自從他有了電話以後，他們就很少見面聊天了。



IV.用 Location+Verb 着 +Noun Phrase 句式改寫下面的句子：

1.有三個房客住在那個公寓裡。

    （住）：那個公寓裡＿＿＿＿＿＿＿＿＿＿＿＿＿＿＿＿＿

2.有幾個人坐在公園的草地上。

    （坐）：公園的草地上＿＿＿＿＿＿＿＿＿＿＿＿＿＿＿

3.客廳的桌子上有一個電視機。

    （放）：客廳的桌子上＿＿＿＿＿＿＿＿＿＿＿＿＿＿

4.門上有一張工作時間表。

    （貼）：門上＿＿＿＿＿＿＿＿＿＿＿＿＿＿＿＿＿＿

# 閱讀練習

Read the following passage within 6 minutes and try to answer the questions before the second reading.

　　小林今天很高興，因為她總算找到一間她滿意的房子了，再過兩個星期她就可以離開現在這個讓她頭疼的地方了。一年前小林因為轉學從費城搬到紐約來，住在皇后區的一個公寓樓裡。這個社區住着很多中國人，所以也有很多中國餐館和中國人開的超級市場，可以説什麼中式食品都有，這對吃不慣西餐的小林來説真是再好不過了！當然小林決定住在這裡的原因主要是因為租金不貴，這樣小林可以省一點錢付學費。

　　可是在這裡住了沒多久小林就開始頭疼了。一是這裡離學校遠，交通也不太方便。每天到學校去得先坐公共車，然後再轉兩次地鐵，結果路上的時間來回就得花近四個小時。二是小林對和她合住的幾個人不太滿意。除了小林以外這裡還住着兩個中國人，一個是女的，是附近一個商店的店員，她好象總有説不完的話，不是找小林聊天，就是在走道上給朋友打電話，一打就是一兩個鐘頭，而且有時打着打着會突然大笑起來，讓小林沒法安安靜靜地看書。另外一個是男的，是在餐館打工的，每天回來得很晚，可是一回來總是把錄音機開得很響，一邊聽流行歌曲一邊大聲地跟着唱，好像不唱幾句就睡不着覺，結果吵得別人沒法睡覺。另外，這兩個人從來不按時打掃公用的地方，廚房、衛生間常常很髒，加上廚房和衛生間裡都沒有窗戶，空氣常常不新鮮，使小林越住越不舒服。

　　兩個星期前小林收到了學校給她的回信，説已經同意給她獎學金了。小林興奮極了，馬上開始到學校附近去找房子，沒有幾天小林就找到了。雖然房租比原來的貴，可是她可以不用每天為坐車轉車花時間了。另外，她的房間的窗戶很大，不但光綫很好，而且空氣也很流通，出了公寓樓往左拐，往前走幾步就是一個圖書館，對面就是郵局。從郵局再往前走一點就是一條大街，大街的兩邊還有商店、咖啡館、超級市場等等，真是再方便不過了！加上離她公寓樓不遠的地方還有一個很不錯的公園，她可以每天都到公園去跑步、運動！……小林越想越興奮：她真希望能儘快開始一個新的生活！

回答問題：
1. 這篇短文説的是什麼？
2. 小林來紐約後住在哪裡？為什麼？她有些什麼麻煩？
3. 小林為什麼對剛找到的房子特別滿意？請畫出來她的公寓樓附近有些什麼。
4. 你有過租房子的經歷(experience)嗎？請談一下你租房子時什麼對你最重要？為什麼？

# 口語練習

I.請你用自己的話說明下面這些詞的意思：
 小吃店；好地區；定金；囉嗦

II.情景會話

練習一：向朋友介紹環境
　　　　有一個中國朋友剛來，不熟悉這裡的環境，想請你介紹一下。你告訴他附近有些什麼，如：超級市場、飯館、商店、郵局、銀行、車站、酒吧、公園、等等。（請你多用學過的句型和詞彙。）

練習二：請你說出來大為、雅克、瑪麗分別應該怎麼走？

　（從地鐵出來......）

1.大為要到郵局去寄信。
2.雅克要先到銀行去，然後再到酒吧去。
3.瑪麗要到新華書店去。
4.最後他們一起坐48路公共汽車去朋友家。

　　　有用的句型和詞彙：
出了地鐵站往＿＿＿走
往前走幾步就有一個＿＿＿＿＿＿
街角上有一個＿＿＿＿＿
一直往前走/（不）過街
走到十字路口往＿＿＿＿＿拐
（要去的地方）就在＿＿＿＿對面（或旁邊）
＿＿＿＿的旁邊（或對面）就是（要去的地方）

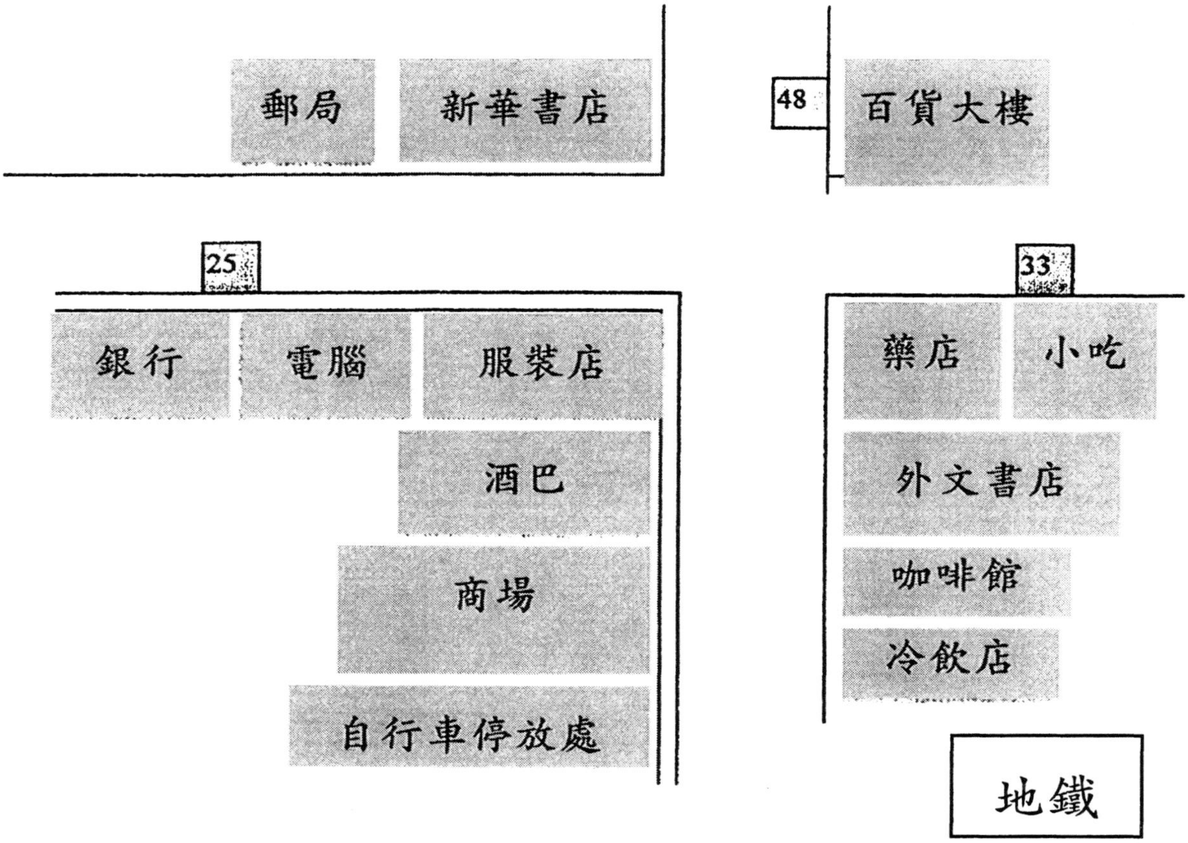

郵局　　新華書店

48 百貨大樓

25

銀行　　電腦　　服裝店

酒巴

商場

自行車停放處

33

藥店　　小吃

外文書店

咖啡館

冷飲店

地鐵

Notes:

大爲 _____

雅克 _____

瑪麗 _____

三人一起 _____

# 寫作練習

假設你是房東或經紀人(broker)，你怎麼向人描述你的房子？（選下面的
一組圖）

## 有用的詞彙：

光綫 [guāngxiàn] lighting     明亮 [míngliàng] bright     寬敞 [kuānchang] spacious

沙發 [shāfā] sofa     茶几 [chájī] tea table /coffee table     空氣 [kōngqì] air

後院 [hòuyuàn] backyard     景色 [jǐngsè] view

# "讓我們好好地樂一樂"

## —過中秋節—

第八課

| Situation | Structure | Culture |
|-----------|-----------|---------|
| 語言情景 | 語言結構 | 文化介紹 |

It's back to Beijing in this lesson, where, in the month of October, it's the time for the Mid-Autumn Festival ( Zhōngqiū jié, 中秋節 ). 大為 and friends go shopping to prepare for the festival activities, and you'll take the opportunity to learn about the customs associated with this very festive time of year.

In terms of grammar, you'll look at "passive" structures, this time using the word 受 (shòu).

Culturally, you'll learn a few things about the Mid-Autumn Festival when the Chinese people are at their most lively and there are lots of good things to eat, such as "mooncakes" (月餅) pictured above.

# "讓我們好好地樂一樂"
## --過中秋節--

中秋晚會！！

同學們，中秋節到了！在這個親人好友團聚的日子裡，

你們一定很想念自己的親友吧？歡迎你來參加我們的晚會：

吃一吃、喝一喝、跳跳舞、唱唱歌、交交朋友、.....讓我們

好好地樂一樂！

時間：星期日晚七時　　地點：中文系大樓110室

　　中秋節到了，中文系的老師和學生們邀請外國留學生們去參加他們的中秋節晚會。大爲他們幾個留學生[i]都很高興。他們都知道中秋節聚會是吃的聚會，所以決定先一起上街去買些食品和飲料。

食品店）

售貨員：你們好，想買點什麼[ii]？

雅克：我們想買點中秋節吃的東西，
　　　就是那個叫什麼——對了——
　　　——"月亮餅"什麼的。

售貨員：噢(O)，你說的是月餅吧？

雅克：對對對，月餅月餅，我們要——
　　　——哎呀，你們說要幾個啊？

瑪麗：我們有幾個人就要幾個。
　　　——六個吧，一人一個

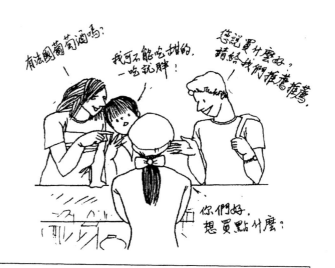

i. "大爲他們幾個留學生..." ("David and his (fellow) foreign students") is a usage-exapmle of two nouns or noun phrases placed next to each other which are said to be "in apposition" to one another. One phrase is the explanatory equivalent of the other. Here are some examples:
我們兩個人 the two of us
大爲、雅克兩個人 the two of them, David and Jacques
這位是我的同學李大爲。 This is Li Dawei, my classmate.

ii. "想買點什麼" is a conventional phrase corresponding to English "Can I help you?" or "How can I help you (buy something)?". Note that Chinese does not have a general phrase like "Can I help you" when offering service. Instead, phrases such as "（您）想買點什麼" or "想吃點什麼" or "（您）有什麼事" are used according to the specific situation.

| 樂 | 乐 | lè | V to have fun, amuse oneself |
|---|---|---|---|
| 過 | 过 | guò | V to observe (a holiday, birthday, etc.) |
| 節 | 节 | jié | BF holiday, festival |
| 過節 | 过节 | guò//jié | VO to observe the holiday |
| 中秋節 | 中秋节 | zhōngqiūjié | N The Moon Festival (lit. "mid-autumn festival" (15th day of the 8th lunar month)) |
| 會 | 会 | huì | N meeting, conference, party |
| 晚會 | 晚会 | wǎnhuì | N evening party |
| 團聚 | 团聚 | tuánjù | V to get together, reunite |
| 日子 | | rìzi | N (special) day(birthday, anniversary, etc.) |
| 想念 | | xiǎngniàn | V [formal] to miss, long for |
| 參加 | 参加 | cānjiā | V to participate, join |
| 跳舞 | | tiào//wǔ | VO to dance |
| 時 | 时 | shí | TW o'clock  (formal use of 點鐘) |
| 地點 | 地点 | dìdiǎn | N location, place (of an event) |
| 系 | | xì | N department (in a college) |
| 邀請 | 邀请 | yāoqǐng | V/N to invite; invitation |
| 聚會 | 聚会 | jùhuì | V/N to get together; get-together, assembly, party |
| -品 | | -pǐn | BF -stuff, item ( Noun-Suffix) |
| 食品 | | shípǐn | N food |
| 飲料 | 饮料 | yǐnliào | N beverage |
| 售貨員 | 售货员 | shòuhuòyuán | N store clerk, salesperson |
| 月亮 | | yuèliang | N the moon |
| 餅 | 饼 | bǐng | N cake, pie, cookie |
| 瑪麗 | 玛丽 | Mǎlì | N (transliteration of) Mary, Marie |

大爲：哎呀瑪麗，你是不是想減肥啊？好容易才[iii]吃一次月餅，一個怎麼
　　　夠？最少也得一人兩個！

售貨員：要什麼味兒的？甜的、鹹的都有。

大爲：這個[iv]——我們從來沒吃過，你說買什麼好？請給我們推薦推薦。

售貨員：我覺得這種五仁月餅不錯，是甜的，里面有五種果仁，很受顧客
　　　歡迎。

瑪麗：我可不能吃甜的、有油的，一吃就胖。

雅克：我倒是很喜歡果仁，如果再加點奶油、巧克力就更好。

大爲：雅克，這是中國的月餅，又[v]不是西式糕點，哪裡來的奶油巧克力？

售貨員：你們看這樣好不好：我們有一種用大盒子包裝的，裡面各種味兒
　　　的都有，這樣誰想吃什麼就吃什麼。

瑪麗：好主意，就買這種盒裝的吧。

售貨員：還要點什麼嗎？

雅克：有法國葡萄酒嗎？

瑪麗：欸，我說[vi]雅克，今天是過中國節，我們應該喝中國酒。

雅克：哎呀你不知道，中國酒很厲害，我一喝就醉，一醉就吐，那多
　　　不雅！

大爲：都怪你不能克制自己。那我看就買中國啤酒好了，再來點汽水。

雅克：好，就這樣吧。小姐，麻煩你給我們一打青島啤酒，再要一打可口
　　　可樂。

售貨員：好的。就這些嗎？好，一共是一百二十四塊三毛五。……這是找您
　　　的錢，這是發票。

---

iii. 好容易才...is the same as 好不容易才... (had a hard time before finally...).
Example: 那本書我找了兩天，好（不）容易才找到了。I searched for the book for two days [and had a hard time] before I finally found it.

iv. "這個——" ("Well...", "Uh...") is a kind of pause filler indicating hesitation caused by uncertainty.

v. 又 here is a tonal adverb suggesting what has been said is obviously out of place. The sentence can be roughly translated as "It is not a Western [style] cake to begin with!" More examples:
你別想騙我，我又不是小孩！ Don't try to fool me; [to begin with] I'm no kid!!
你又不是他，你怎麼知道他不喜歡？ You're not HIM! How do you know he doesn't like it?

vi. "我說，..." is often used as an initiator to draw the attention of others to one's message, similar to English 'Hey', "Listen,...","Look,..." or "Let me tell you something:...".

| 減 | 减 | jiǎn | V to reduce, deduct, minus |
| 減肥 | 减肥 | jiǎnféi | VO to go on diet ("reduce fat") |
| 甜 | | tián | ADJ sweet |
| 鹹 | 咸 | xián | ADJ salty |
| 推薦 | 推荐 | tuījiàn | V/N to recommend; recommendation |
| 果仁 | | guǒrén | N nuts |
| 受 | | shòu | V/CV to receive; by (see Structural Focus) |
| 顧客 | 顾客 | gùkè | N customer, client |
| 油 | | yóu | ADJ/N oily, greasy; oil, grease |
| 倒(是) | | dàoshì | A actually, on the other hand |
| 巧克力 | | qiǎokèlì | N (transliteration of) chocolate |
| 奶油 | | nǎiyóu | N butter, cream |
| 糕點 | 糕点 | gāodiǎn | N pastry |
| 盒子 | | hézi | N box |
| 包裝 | 包装 | bāozhuāng | V to pack, packaging |
| 盒裝(的) | 盒装(的) | hézhuāng(de) | box-packed; boxed |
| 蛋糕 | | dàngāo | N layer cake; cake |
| 葡萄 | | pútao | N grapes |
| 醉 | | zuì | V to get drunk; drunk |
| 青島 | 青岛 | Qīngdǎo | N (name of a Chinese city in Shandong, famous for its beer, often exported abroad) |
| 啤酒 | | píjiǔ | N beer |
| 打 | | dá | M a dozen (note tone!) |
| 汽水 | | qìshuǐ | N soda (carbonated beverage) |
| 可口可樂 | 可口可乐 | Kěkǒu Kělè | N (transliteration of) Coca Cola |
| 找錢 | 找钱 | zhǎo//qián | VO to give change |
| 發票 | 发票 | fāpiào | N (sales) receipt |

判斷出以下詞語的意思：

食品店
各種味兒　　　　各种味儿

大為等：謝謝。

售貨員：不謝。歡迎以後再來。

......

　　中秋節晚會很熱鬧。大家吃吃玩玩、唱唱跳跳，高高興興地玩了一晚上。大為最興奮的是他新交了幾個中國朋友。這是他來到中國後最輕鬆的一天，他開始喜歡這裡的生活了。

| 熱鬧 | 热闹 | rènao | ADJ (atmosphere) festive, lively, noisy |
| 輕鬆 | 轻松 | qīngsōng | ADJ light-hearted, relaxed, easy |

回答問題：

1. 中秋節是一個什麼樣的節日？在什麼時候？
2. 中秋晚會是誰主辦 (host) 的？為什麼要邀請其他學生參加？
3. 晚會上大為最高興的是什麼事？為什麼說"他開始喜歡這裡的生活了"？

## Using Shòu 受 Constructions for Passive Voice

受 (shòu) is one of several words in Chinese that can be used to express the passive tone. 受 implies a passive meaning in that it suggests "receiving" as opposed to "giving" or "generating". Because of this implied passivity 受 sentences are often translated by the passive voice in English. But unlike other passive markers, such as 被 (bèi), which we will practice in a future lesson, and which is used essentially to express an adverse or unfortunate situation, 受 is used in positive senses as well. 受 sentences can take various forms depending on the focus of their message. When preceded by 很 or 不, the 受 sentence usually refers to a general situation or status. But when a specific event or matter during a particular time frame is the concern, 受到 is more likely to be used. The words used as the object of 受 is typically abstract, for example, "popularity," "favor," "attention," "influence," "education," "respect," and the like. Here are some examples:

### A. General comment on current situation/status during a particular time frame
- 這本書很受歡迎。 This book is/has been very popular.
- 這本書不太受歡迎。 This book is/has not been very popular.

### B. Specific event/status at a particular time
- 這本書出來以後受到很大的歡迎。 After the book came out it was well received.
- 當時這本書沒受到歡迎。 The book was poorly received at that time.

Note:
- Type A uses 不 for negation
- Use 沒 for negation in Type B sentences.
- 很 cannot be used before 受到

### C. Specifying source:
In both types above, 受 can be followed by a noun phrase to indicate the source of the attention, popularity, respect, etc. Here are some examples:
- 這本書很受學生歡迎。 This book is very popular among students.
- 這本書受到很多中國人（的）重視。 Many Chinese have a high regard for this book/This book has received the attention of many Chinese.

# 辭彙用法
## Word Usage

### Verbs
- 團聚：跟親人團聚；每年團聚一次；他們團聚了三天又分開了。
- 想念：想念親友；想念家鄉 (jiāxiāng: hometown)；想念得很厲害
- 參加：參加晚會；參加活動；參加過三次晚會；今天的晚會有三十個人參加。
- 邀請：邀請朋友；邀請他們來參加晚會（吃飯、玩幾天）。
- 推薦：推薦工作；推薦一個人；請你給我推薦推薦。/我推薦你買這種月餅
- 醉：你（喝）醉了。/我沒醉。/醉得很厲害
- 過：過節（生日、週末、星期天、生活...）；生日過得怎麼樣？/過得很沒意思

### Verb-Object Compounds
- 找錢：這是找您的錢。/找三塊錢；找錯錢了；你應該找（給）我五塊錢。
- 過節：過中秋節(情人節、母親節...)；跟中國人一起過節。/過節過得很開心

### Adjectives
- 熱鬧：晚會很熱鬧。/這條街白天很熱鬧。/熱鬧得不得了；熱熱鬧鬧地過節
- 輕鬆：他的生活很輕鬆 (carefree, easy)。/這次的考試很輕鬆 (easy)。/考完試以後，大家都覺得很輕鬆。/我喜歡輕鬆的音樂。

### Appositives (See Text Notes # 1)
- 大為他們幾個留學生；大為雅克兩個人；他們幾個人走了沒有？
- 這是我的新朋友小李。/我們中國人都愛唱這個歌。

### Nouns
- 日子：今天是什麼日子？/中秋節是親人團聚的日子。/後天是他結婚的日子。
- 聚會：今天我們系裡有個聚會。/很有意思的聚會；很大的聚會
- 地點：聚會的地點；見面的地點；這個地點不太好（不方便、 太遠...）

**1.**受...；受到...（歡迎，重視，喜愛...）**(...received [popularity, attention, favor, etc.])**

- 這個商店很受顧客歡迎。This store is/has been very popular with customers.
- 這個商店受到顧客（的）歡迎。This store has been well-received by customers.
- 這件事不受大家重視。This matter is not taken seriously by people.
- 這件事沒有受到大家（的）重視。This matter did not receive much attention from people.
- 中國菜 _____
- He is the least popular person here.

- The economy of East Asia is attracting more and more attention.

**2.Sb. ...(QW-form) 就 ...(QW-form) ( sb. does whatever sb. wants to ... )**

- 誰想吃什麼就吃什麼吧。Anyone can eat whatever he/she wants.
- 他想跟誰結婚就跟誰結婚。He can marry anyone he wants.
- 我不想管你的事，你想去哪裡就去哪裡吧。
- 你別客氣，_____
- I have money now. I can buy whatever I want and as much as I like.

- Just say whatever you want to say.

**3.**就 V 好了 **( Why don't you just...... )**

- 我叫李大爲，你就叫我大爲好了。My name is Li Dawei. Why don't you just call me Dawei.
- 你就在這兒待着好了，我馬上回來。
- 甲：我們今天中午吃什麼？乙：_____
- I won't be home tomorrow. Just put the book in my doorway.

**4. 都怪......** ( It's all sb's fault that...; Sb. is to blame )

* 你一喝酒就醉，都怪你不會克制自己。You get drunk every time you drink and you are the one to blame because you don't know how to control yourself.

* 他的兒子跑了 (ran away)。都怪他管孩子管得太嚴。

* 我們昨天玩得不高興，_____

* I didn't do well on the exam yesterday and it's all my fault because I didn't really prepare for it.

**5. 好(不)容易才 V** ( had great difficulty before finally... )

* 我找了幾個月，好(不)容易才找到一個滿意的公寓。 I looked for an apartment for months [and had a hard time] before I finally found a satisfactory one.

* 我們好(不)容易才有機會跟中國人一塊過節，當然應該熱熱鬧鬧地過。

* 他忙了半天，_____

* 我_____，所以這兩天想好好休息一下。

**6. 你看(說、覺得)(Sb.) V...好 ？ (What would you suggest?/What [where, etc.] do you think [sb.] should ...?)**

* 我想買一點兒吃的東西，你看（我）買什麼好？
  I'd like to buy some food. What do you think/suggest/recommend I should buy?

* 我想自己學中文，你說（我）用什麼書好？

* 今天去參加他的生日晚會，你覺得 _____?

* I want to throw a party on Friday. Whom do you think I should invite?

# 文化介紹
## Learning About Culture
### 過中秋節
**Celebrating the Mid-Autumn Festival**

The very popular Zhōngqiū jié 中秋節 or Mid-Autumn Festival, also known as the Moon Festival, 八月節, takes place on the 15th day of the 8th month (approx. late September or early October), around harvest time, when the weather is often at its best, neither too hot nor too cold. The moon is full at this time and at its brightest. 大為 and friends look forward to moon-gazing and eating tasty moon cakes (月餅), popular pastimes at this festive time of year.

Since this is harvest time it is, of course, the happiest month of the year for farmers. For the rest of the nation, it is also one of the most joyous occasions. Yet another name for this festival is Tuányuán Jié 團圓節, "The Festival of Re-unions." With the air extraordinarily clear, the full, especially bright round moon symbolizes a happy, complete family "circle," appropriate to this occasion when tradition dictates that all members of the family have a reunion and enjoy each other's company. People usually celebrate at night, outdoors in the moonlight, chatting, joking and sipping wine. The Chinese call these activities shǎngyuè 賞月 "admiring the moon-light."

The Mid-Autumn moon has been the subject of thousands of literary works; the activities associated with shǎngyuè 賞月, likewise, are the subject of many folk tales. One such story,

telling about the custom of eating moon-cakes, has remained a favorite of the Chinese for generations. The legend goes back to the Yuan Dynasty (1271-1368) when the Mongols ruled China with literally an "iron" hand. In order to control any iron which the Chinese might use to forge weapons to rebel, the Mongol court issued a decree that only one knife would be available for every ten households. Furthermore, every ten households also had to feed and lodge one Mongol soldier. Among the Chinese people who were brutally treated by the Mongol, some finally plotted to revolt. One year, just before the Mid-Autumn Festival, a group of them made a tremendous number of round cakes, in each of which was inserted a written message. The cakes were then distributed to each household as festival gifts. They were supposed to be eaten at a specific time on the morning of the Mid-Autumn Festival. When finally every household opened the cakes, a startling message was revealed. It said, "All of us, let us kill the Mongols now!" The Chinese rose in rebellion, threw out the alien rulers and once again established Chinese rule of China. Eating mooncakes, without accompanying revolution, however, has become a custom at the Mid-Autumn Festival ever since.

## 第一部分：單句

請你們聽下面的句子。每個句子的意思是什麼？請在三個選擇中選出一句來。
Listen to the recorded statements. Circle the sentence from the three choices which is closest in meaning to the statement heard.

1.　(a)老師越嚴格越不受歡迎。
　　(b)嚴格的老師一定受人歡迎。
　　(c)學生可能會喜歡嚴格的老師。

2.　(a)我們吃了你推薦的巧克力就瘦了。
　　(b)我們很喜歡你推薦的巧克力。
　　(c)我們對你推薦的巧克力不滿意。

3.　(a)你什麼時候做功課都不要緊。
　　(b)如果你不按時做功課，我就會不高興。
　　(c)你還是趕快把功課做好吧。

4.　(a)你可以藉着中秋節的機會回去和家人團聚。
　　(b)中秋節的時候你可以參加同學的聚會。
　　(c)中秋節是一個使人想念親友的日子。

5.　(a)我這幾個星期來吃的奶油蛋糕很奇怪。
　　(b)我很不高興自己又吃胖了。
　　(c)我希望長得胖一點兒，所以吃了好多奶油蛋糕。

6.　(a)打掃房子是件很簡單的事，我一下子就做好了。
　　(b)打掃房子不是件輕鬆的事，我忙了半天才做好。
　　(c)我每天都忙着打掃房子。

7.　(a)你覺得我應該送他什麼吃的東西？
　　(b)我知道吃什麼食品能幫助他減肥。
　　(c)他喜歡什麼食品我就送他什麼食品。

## 第二部分：對話

第一遍：下面是海琳和她的房東楊小姐的對話。請你們聽懂這個對話的大意，然後回答問題。

First Listening: Listen to the recorded dialogue between Hailin and her landlady Miss Yang. Try to get a general idea of what it is about. After you listen, answer these questions.

問題：1.海琳和楊小姐在說些什麼？

      a)開晚會的事         b)中秋節的事

    2.海琳今年決定在哪兒過中秋？

      a)伯父母家         b)楊小姐家

第二遍：請你們讀下面的句子。然後把這個對話再聽一次。聽完後，看看這些句子說得對不對。

Second Listening: Read the following statements. Then listen to the dialogue again. After you listen, decide whether the statements are true or false.

_____ 1.中秋節那天，海琳跟楊小姐要在她們的公寓裡開一個晚會。

_____ 2.海琳的伯父、伯母希望她回去跟他們一塊過節。

_____ 3.中秋節對海琳的家人來說，是一個很重要的日子。

_____ 4.中秋節正好是海琳的生日。

_____ 5.海琳已經買好了月餅，準備中秋節當天帶到伯父家去。

_____ 6.海琳希望楊小姐能為她出個主意，看買什麼月餅好。

# 第八課 練習

## 辭彙；句型；語法

I.<u>填空</u>：

1.<u>過</u>：過＿＿＿＿＿節；過節過＿＿＿＿＿很快樂；中國人過＿＿＿＿的時候

　　　　吃麵條，西方人吃蛋糕。/上個星期天你＿＿＿＿＿＿＿＿＿＿＿＿＿＿？

2.<u>參加</u>：參加＿＿＿＿＿＿；我們系裡的活動，你＿＿＿＿＿＿沒有？

3.<u>邀請</u>：邀請＿＿＿＿＿＿＿；謝謝＿＿＿＿＿，我一定來參加你的生日晚會。

4.<u>推薦</u>：推薦＿＿＿＿＿；我請老師給我寫一封＿＿＿＿＿＿＿＿＿＿＿＿＿。

　　　　/我不知道買什麼好，你給我＿＿＿＿＿＿＿＿＿＿。

5.<u>想念</u>：想念＿＿＿＿＿＿；我＿＿＿＿＿＿的時候最想念＿＿＿＿＿＿。

6.<u>輕鬆</u>：＿＿＿＿＿＿很輕鬆。/我現在覺得很（不）輕鬆，因為＿＿＿＿＿＿。

7.＿＿＿＿＿品；＿＿＿＿＿品；＿＿＿＿＿式；＿＿＿＿＿式；

8.<u>熱鬧</u>：＿＿＿＿＿＿＿＿很熱鬧。/他喜歡住在＿＿＿＿＿＿＿＿。

II.<u>完成句子</u>：

1.我查了半天，好不容易才＿＿＿＿＿＿＿＿＿＿＿＿＿＿＿＿＿。

2.我對我住的那個地區不太滿意，都怪＿＿＿＿＿＿＿＿＿＿＿＿＿＿＿。

3.明天是你的生日聚會，你想＿＿＿＿＿＿＿就＿＿＿＿＿＿＿＿。

4.我下星期沒有課，想出去玩玩，你說＿＿＿＿＿＿＿＿＿＿＿好？

5.你如果想輕鬆一下，交幾個朋友，那明天就＿＿＿＿＿＿＿＿＿好了。

III.<u>用"受"字結構改寫下面的句子</u>:很（不）受......　　（沒）受到......

（歡迎）

學生都很喜歡那個老師。　＿＿＿＿＿＿＿＿＿＿＿＿＿＿＿＿＿＿＿＿

美國人很喜歡這種衣服。　＿＿＿＿＿＿＿＿＿＿＿＿＿＿＿＿＿＿＿＿

這种糕點很少有人買。　　＿＿＿＿＿＿＿＿＿＿＿＿＿＿＿＿＿＿＿＿

（重視、注意）

現在大家都認爲東亞經濟很重要。＿＿＿＿＿＿＿＿＿＿＿＿＿＿＿＿＿

以前人們沒有重視這種病的原因。＿＿＿＿＿＿＿＿＿＿＿＿＿＿＿＿＿

再過兩年就會有更多的人注意他的這個新發現。

＿＿＿＿＿＿＿＿＿＿＿＿＿＿＿＿＿＿＿＿＿＿＿＿＿＿＿＿＿＿＿＿

# 閱讀練習

## 過中秋節

　　我記得小時候我最喜歡過的就是中秋節。因爲這一天我和哥哥弟弟都能吃到很多好吃的東西，還可以聽爸爸媽媽講中秋節的故事。<u>離</u>中秋節<u>還有一個星期</u>1的時候，媽媽就開始<u>做過節的準備</u>2了：買月餅、水果等等。媽媽買來了月餅以後不讓我們吃，説要等到中秋節才能吃。所以我和哥哥弟弟都盼着中秋節早一點到。<u>好不容易</u>3盼到中秋節了，這一天晚飯我們都吃得很少，因爲吃多了就<u>吃不下</u>4月餅了。左等右等總算等到天黑了，這時媽媽把準備好的食品都拿出來了：啊！一大桌好吃的東西，<u>光</u>5月餅就有七八種！另外還有新鮮水果、<u>玉米</u>6、<u>花生</u>7、<u>等等</u>8。我們一家人高高興興地坐在<u>院子</u>9裡，一邊吃東西，一邊看月亮。這一天的月亮特別<u>圓</u>10特別亮，月亮上好像有一<u>棵樹</u>11，有一個人，還有一隻小白<u>兔</u>12。這時爸爸媽媽就會給我們講<u>嫦娥</u>13的故事……

　　很早很早以前有一個名叫后羿(hòuyì)的人，他有一個很美的<u>妻子</u>14，名叫嫦娥。后羿<u>得到</u>15了一包藥，<u>據説</u>16吃了這個藥人就會飛到<u>天上</u>17去，<u>永遠</u>18不會死了。可是后羿不願意離開嫦娥自己飛到天上去，所以就沒有吃這個藥。有一天，不知道怎麼搞的，嫦娥把這個藥吃了，馬上就覺得身子<u>輕飄飄</u>19地飛起來，<u>一直</u>20飛到月亮上去了。后羿發現後趕快去<u>追</u>21，可是太晚了。后羿<u>抬頭</u>22看天上，看見嫦娥在月亮上看着他，知道她一定很想他，所以他就在院子裡放了一桌嫦娥最愛吃的水果，<u>遠遠地</u>23和嫦娥聚會。以後每年的這一天他都這樣跟嫦娥<u>團圓</u>24，所以這一天月亮也就特別圓特別亮，人們也就把這一天叫團圓節。

<u>生詞表</u>（請把空着的詞彙的意思查出來）：

| | | |
|---|---|---|
| 1.離…還有… _____ | 9.院子 [yuànzi] courtyard | 17.天上 _____ |
| 2.做…準備 make preparations for | 10.圓 [yuán] round; (the moon) full | 18.永遠 _____ |
| 3.好不容易 _____ | 11.棵 [kē] (measure for trees, plants) | 19.輕飄飄 [qīngpiāopiāo] lightly |
| 4.吃不下 _____ | 12.兔 [tù] rabbit | 20.一直 _____ |
| 5.光 [guāng] just | 13.嫦娥 [cháng é] | 21.追 [zhuī] chase |
| 6.玉米 [yùmǐ] corn | 14.妻子 [qīzi] wife | 22.抬頭 [tái tóu] lift the head |
| 7.花生 [huāshēng] peanuts | 15.得到 _____ | 23.遠遠地 _____ |
| 8.等等 _____ | 16.據説 [jùshuō] it is said | 24.團圓 _____ |

回答問題：

1. 爲什麼作者 (zuòzhě: author) 最喜歡過中秋節？爲什麼要盼着中秋節早到？

2. 中秋節的時候他們吃些什麼？在哪裡吃？爲什麼？

3. 嫦娥是什麼人？她爲什麼會在月亮上？

4. 爲什麼中秋節也叫團圓節？

## 口語練習

I. 補充詞彙 (請大聲唸兩遍)：

1. 香蕉 [xiāngjiāo] banana
2. 草莓 [cǎoméi] strawberry
3. 葡萄 [pútao] grapes
4. 蘋果 [píngguǒ] apple
5. 桃子 [táozi] peach
6. 芒果 [mángguǒ] mango
7. 牛奶 [niúnǎi] cow's milk
8. 冰淇淋 [bīngqilín] ice cream
9. 酸奶 [suānnǎi] yogurt
10. 啤酒 [píjiǔ] beer
11. 橙汁 [chéngzhī] orange juice
12. 七喜 [qīxǐ] 7 up
13. 可口可樂 [kěkǒukělè] Coca Cola
14. 雪碧 [xuěbì] Sprite
15. 百事可樂 [bǎishìkělè] Pepsi
16. 礦泉水 [kuàngquánshuǐ] spring water

II. 回答下面的問題：

1. 香蕉（蘋果、葡萄）是什麼顏色？樣子？味道？在哪兒可以買到？
2. 哪些水果是圓的？甜的？哪些是酸的(suān:sour)？
3. 你喜歡喝哪種果汁？你覺得哪些果汁最受歡迎？
4. 汽水和礦泉水哪一種喝了對身體好？你喜歡喝哪種汽水？（可口可樂、百事可樂、雪碧）
5. 啤酒喝了會不會醉？你喜歡喝什麼啤酒？喝過青島啤酒嗎？
6. 你跟朋友聚會的時候都愛買什麼食品和飲料？

III. 情景會話：買食品飲料

　　你和朋友要開一個生日聚會，所以到食品店去買食品和飲料。（三人一組練習，其中一個人當售貨員。對話中包括問價格、請售貨員推薦、最後決定買什麼食品和飲料。）

IV. 敘述練習：過感恩節 (Gǎn ēn jié: Thanksgiving Day)

請看下面的圖，然後把整個事情敘述出來。

有用的詞語：

超級市場[chāojíshìchǎng] supermarket　火雞[huǒjī]turkey　　　遊行[yóuxíng]parade
熱鬧[rènao]festive, exciting　　　　客人[kèren] guests　　　餐桌[cānzhuō]dinner table
圍著....坐[wéizhe...zuò]sit around ...　晚餐[wǎncān]dinner

# 寫作練習

1.<u>談過節</u>：

　　　　—你最喜歡過的是什麼節？為什麼？

　　　　—過這個節的時候大家都做些什麼、吃些什麼？

　　　　—你今年是怎麼過的（或者打算怎麼過）這個節日？

2.<u>看圖習作</u>：請把上面〔口語練習〕裡<u>過感恩節</u>的事寫出來。

　　　感恩節到了，同學們都要回家去過節，可是中國留學生小張在美國沒有親戚朋友，所以看樣子只好一個人留在宿舍裡了。她的同屋瑪麗看她很寂寞，就......

_____

_____

_____

_____

_____

_____

......就這樣，小張在瑪麗家過了一個愉快的感恩節。

# "歡迎你到我們公司來工作"
## —工作面試—

第九課

| Situation | Structure | Culture |
|---|---|---|
| 語言情景 | 語言結構 | 文化介紹 |

海琳 continues in this lesson to strike out on her own: now she's looking for a job and you'll join her in her first job interview and take the opportunity to learn some language useful in a situation in which you may find yourself one day.

As far as structure is concerned, you'll take a look at a familiar word: 有. We find out how 有 can combine to form many compound words common in modern Chinese.

And culturally, you'll learn a few things about how Chinese job applicants behave during a job interview and how such behavior reflects wider concepts of modesty and behavior in China.

# "歡迎你到我們公司來工作"
## --工作面試[i]--

　　海琳在報上看到一個廣告。有一家進出口公司，要僱一位負責北美市場的業務代表，條件是大專畢業、中英文流利、熱情、有工作經驗；月薪24,000元起。海琳對這個工作很感興趣，雖然她並沒有進出口工作的經驗，可是她打算去試試看，於是她馬上跟這個公司聯絡。公司叫她帶着履歷表去面試。跟海琳面談的是公司的經理[ii]，海琳有一點緊張。

經理：吳小姐，我們看了你的履歷了。你的學歷和英文我們都很滿意，中文說得也很流利。不過你的中文閱讀和書寫能力好像不夠強。

i. 面試 literally means "face-to-face test" and should not be used for interviews such as those used to cover a news story, a research interview, etc. Reserve this word for 'job interview.' There is no single Chinese word equivalent to the English word "interview" in a general sense.

ii. The position of 經理 in a Chinese administrative system involves a high-ranking officer, often the head (president or vice-president) of a company or administrative unit. The English translation, 'manager,' does not convey this sense of high rank.

| | | | |
|---|---|---|---|
| 公司 | | gōngsī | N company |
| 面試 | 面试 | miànshì | V/N to have a (job) interview; (job) interview |
| 進口 | 进口 | jìnkǒu | V/N to import; import |
| 出口 | | chūkǒu | V/N to export; export |
| 僱(用) | 雇(用) | gùyòng | V to hire (for employment) |
| 負責 | 负责 | fùzé | V be responsible (for), in charge of |
| 市場 | 市场 | shìchǎng | N market |
| 業務 | 业务 | yèwù | N business activities, field stuff |
| 代表 | | dàibiǎo | V/N to represent; representative |
| 大專 | 大专 | dàzhuān | N university & professional school (abbr. of 大學 and 專科學校/专科学校 zhuānkē xuéxiào) |
| 流利 | | liúlì | ADJ fluent |
| 經驗 | 经验 | jīngyàn | N experience |
| 薪水 | | xīnshuǐ | N salary |
| 月薪 | | yuè xīn | N monthly salary |
| 興趣 | 兴趣 | xìngqù | N interest (in sth.) |
| 感興趣 | 感兴趣 | gǎn xìngqù | VP be interested |
| 於是 | 于是 | yúshì | CONJ so, then, thereupon, therefore |
| 聯絡 | 联络 | liánluò | V/N to get in touch; contact (between people) |
| 表 | | biǎo | N chart, table, list, form |
| 履歷表 | 履历表 | lǚlìbiǎo | N resume, curriculum vitae |
| 面談 | 面谈 | miàntán | V/N to talk face-to-face; face-to-face talk |
| 經理 | 经理 | jīnglǐ | N (business) manager (see notes) |
| 緊張 | 紧张 | jǐnzhāng | ADJ nervous, tense |
| 學歷 | 学历 | xuélì | N educational background |
| 閱讀 | 阅读 | yuèdú | V/N. to read; reading |
| 書寫 | 书写 | shūxiě | N [formal] writing (skill) |
| 能力 | | nénglì | N ability, capability (abbr. as 力 in compounds) |
| 強 | 强 | qiáng | ADJ strong, powerful |

海琳：我的讀寫是稍差一點，主要是因爲我不太熟悉中文的商業術語，如果有本商業字典，再多練習練習也就熟了，我想問題不大<sup>iii</sup>。如果你們公司想找的業務代表主要是用英文，那我還是很有信心的。

經理：你過去有沒有做過進出口方面的工作？

海琳：沒有，不过我在美國的時候曾經做過一段時間的產品推銷業務助理，我想這可能會很有幫助的，而且我也會用商業電腦。當然主要是我對這個工作特別有興趣，很想在這方面發展發展。我相信我會很快熟悉這裡的業務的，希望經理能給我一個機會試試。

經理：嗯(ng)——你看這樣好不好：業務代表這個職務需要很有經驗的人，你可能還需要一些訓練才行。不過呢，我們這裡正好也想找一個業務助理，你可以先試試這個工作。薪水稍低一點，但你可以藉這個機會學一下。等你熟悉這裡的業務了我們可以再請你做業務代表，你看怎麼樣？

海琳：太好了！謝謝經理。

經理：不客氣。非常歡迎你到我們公司來工作！

海琳：我一定會努力的，請經理放心。

經理：好，我相信你。等一下李秘書會帶你去看看你的辦公室，給你介紹一下我們公司的情況，你有什麼問題就問她好了。下星期你就可以開始上班了。

海琳：好。那就星期一見。

經理：星期一見。

---

iii. "我想問題不大" means "I don't think it'll be a problem."

| 稍微 | | shāowēi | A slightly (can be shortened as 稍 |
| 差 | | chà | ADJ poor (in quality, ability) |
| 主要 | | zhǔyào | MOD/A main, major, essential; mainly, essentially |
| 商業 | 商业 | shāngyè | N business, commerce |
| 術語 | 术语 | shùyǔ | N professional terminology, jargon |
| 字典 | | zìdiǎn | N dictionary |
| 信心 | | xìnxīn | N confidence, faith |
| 過去 | 过去 | guòqù | TW in the past, formerly |
| 做 | | zuò | V to be (a teacher, manager, mother, etc.) |
| 方面 | | fāngmiàn | N aspect, area |
| 曾經 | 曾经 | céngjīng | A (did/was) once, ever |
| 產品 | 产品 | chǎnpǐn | N product |
| 推銷 | 推销 | tuīxiāo | V to (promote and) sell, to market |
| 助理 | | zhùlǐ | N assistant |
| 發展 | 发展 | fāzhǎn | V/N to develop; development |
| 職務 | 职务 | zhíwù | N (job) position |
| 需要 | | xūyào | V/N to need; needs |
| 訓練 | 训练 | xùnliàn | V/N to train; training |
| 秘書 | 秘书 | mìshū | N secretary |
| 上班 | | shàng//bān | VO to go to work, to work (in one's office) |

回答問題：
1.這家公司是做什麼的？他們為什麼要找一個中英文都流利的人？
2.海琳的什麼方面強，什麼方面不強？她是怎麼向經理說自己的能力的？
3.既然海琳的中文能力並不夠強，而且又沒有經驗，那經理為什麼還同意僱她？
4.海琳為什麼願意接受一個低一點的職務？你認為她這個決定做得對不對？

## Using 有 + Abstract Nouns as Verb-Objects and Adjectives

The familiar word 有 can often be compounded with nouns (often abstract) to form words which function as either verb-object phrases or adjectives. This function enables 有-compounds to convey the same meaning in slightly different ways. When a 有-compound is used as an adjective, it is often preceded by an adverb of degree such as 很，非常，or 特別. On the other hand, when the compound is used as a verb-object, other words can be inserted between 有 and the noun. The difference between the two forms is that the adjective form functions as a general comment, while the verb-object form can make the phrase more specific with inserted modifiers. Such usage of 有-compounds is extremely common in the colloquial language but also very common in more formal language situations.

Here's some examples: (note the difference in specific reference)

Adjective:　　　他很（没）有能力。　　He is capable. / He is not capable.
　　　　　　　　這本書對我很有幫助。　This book is/has been very helpful to me.

Verb-Object:　　他在這方面有<u>很強的</u>能力。　　He has strong ability in this area.
(with modifier)　這本書對我有<u>非常大的</u>幫助。　This book has been very helpful to me.
　　　　　　　　這本書對我<u>一點</u>幫助都没有。　This book is no help to me at all.

As an exercise create some sentences using the following 有-compounds in both forms:

有辦法　　　"have solution" —> "resourceful"
有幫助　　　"have help"—> "helpful"
有經驗　　　"have experience" —> "experienced"
有興趣　　　"have interest" —> "interested"
有能力　　　"have ability" —> "able" " capable"
有信心　　　"have confidence/faith" —> "confident"
有希望　　　"have hope" —> "hopeful" "promising"

# 辭彙用法
## Word Usage

### Verbs
- 面試：到公司去面試；面試過幾次；工作面試；參加面試(N)
- 面談：跟經理面談；面談過幾次；在辦公室裡面談
- 負責：我負責打掃客廳。/這件事是他負責。/他做事很負責。(Adj)
- 聯絡：跟朋友聯絡；用電話聯絡；保持聯絡；我們很久沒聯絡了。
- 閱讀：到圖書館去閱讀書報；閱讀能力；閱讀練習；閱讀習慣(Mod.)
- 推銷：推銷產品；他向我們推銷了不少新書。/推銷得很順利；
  推銷員 (salesman)
- 發展：發展經濟；發展得很快；經濟的發展；在經濟方面有很大的
  發展(N)
- 需要：需要很多錢；你需要什麼？/我需要你幫忙。
  顧客的需要；市場需要；有很多需要(N)
- 僱用：僱用一個秘書；我們沒僱用過外國人。/受公司的僱用(N)

### Verb-Object Compounds
- 上班：到公司去上班；你在哪裡上班？/明天不必上班。/上班上得很
  辛苦。/九點上班，五點下班。/上班上到五點；我在那個公司
  上過一年班。

### Adjectives/Adverbs
- 流利：中文說得很流利；他能說一口流利的中文。
- 努力：努力工作；工作得很努力；不夠努力；需要更多的努力(N)
- 稍微：稍微差一點；稍微貴了一些；請你把字稍微寫大一點。
- 強：能力很強；信心很強；對中文的興趣很強；他的中文很強。
- 差：能力很差；產品很差；身體 (health) 很差；字寫得很差

### Nouns
- 代表：業務代表；公司的代表；學生代表；他代表學校參加歌唱
  比賽。(V)
- 經驗：工作經驗；經驗很多；在這方面沒什麼經驗；經驗不夠；很有
  經驗
- 興趣：興趣很大；他的興趣很廣。/他對什麼都感興趣。/我對他很有
  興趣。
- 學歷：學歷很高；大學學歷；我只有高中學歷。
- 能力：辦事能力；書寫能力；能力很強；能力不夠；很有能力(Adj)
- 訓練：你在這方面的訓練不夠。/需要多一點訓練；訓練了一段時間(V)
- 方面：這方面；進出口方面；在經濟方面；在閱讀方面他的能力很強。
- 術語：商業術語；電腦術語；經濟術語；廣告術語
- 信心：信心很強；對這個工作有很大的信心；對這個工作很有信心(Adj)

# 句型和習慣用語
## Sentence Patterns and Expressions

1.對......感/有興趣 ( be interested in...; to take interest in....)
- 我對這個工作很感興趣。 I am very interested in this job.
- 他對流行歌曲沒有興趣，可是我很有興趣。
- 甲：你對什麼最不感興趣？ 乙：_____
- He is not interested in going to parties at all.

2. ......，於是 (sb.) 就 V 了 ...... (..., so/thereupon sb. did sth. [as an immediate
   reaction])
- 那個電腦很好用，而且也不貴，於是我就買了。
  That computer is user-friendly and it's not expensive either, so I bought it.
- 我這段時間在找工作，正好那個公司需要一個秘書，於是我就去申請了。
- 那個公寓的大小對我很合適，而且附近的環境也很好，_____
- 那家食品店不賣這種蛋糕，_____我只好 _____
- He is not used to eating in restaurants, so he cooks at home every day.

**Compare with** 所以： **(used for justification; not necessarily past and immediate effect)**

　　　[為什麼申請那個工作？]那個工作對我很合適，所以我就申請了 or 所以我想申請。

**Compare with** 結果： **(indicating a result which is not necessarily a voluntary reaction or**

**immediate effect)**

　　　他吃東西不注意衛生，結果就生病了。

　　　她考試前認真地複習了功課，結果考得很好

3. 曾經 V 過 ( **ever did sth. in the past** )

- 我曾經在中國待過一段時間。 I once stayed in China for a period of time.
- 我曾經跟他商量過這件事。 I discussed this matter with him.
- 我在大學的時候，_____
- 甲：你以前工作過嗎？乙：在_____ 的時候，我_____。
- I once worked as a sales manager for three months in that company.

4. ...主要是...... ( **mainly...; primarily...** )

- 我們公司想找的業務代表主要是用英文。 The sales representative that our company is looking for will primarily speak and write in English.
- 我決定到台灣去工作，主要是想熟悉熟悉那裡的情況。
- 他想自己租一間房子住，_____
- The reason why I didn't take the apartment is mainly that it is not near stores.

5. ......你看(說，覺得，認為)怎麼樣？ ( **......What do you think?** )

- 我們今天晚上出去吃飯，你看怎麼樣？ Let's eat out tonight. What do you think?
- 我想把這些錢拿來買一套中式傢具，你覺得怎麼樣？
- _____ ，你認為怎麼樣？
- Although I don't have any experience in that area, I'd like to give it a try. What do you think?

# 文化介紹
## Learning About Culture
## 中國人工作面試時的謙卑觀念
## Modesty During a Job Interview

Chinese conceptions about proper behavior are seen in many aspects of daily life and we encounter one in this lesson: the job interview. Chinese sages from Confucius in ancient times, to Lin Yutang in modern times, have recognized the role and necessity of moderation in human affairs. One thinks of the Confucian concept of the 'middle way' or the Doctrine of the Mean. Taoist philosphy speaks at length about the concept of qiān (謙),-- which means moderation or modesty -- a concept that has played a key role in how the Chinese conceive of proper behavior in society.

Now ordinarily a job interview is an opportunity for the applicant to display his/her best stuff, just as a resume is a chance to toot your own personal horn. Nothing wrong with that. But Chinese treat the job interview quite differently. They take care to be modest in speech, dress and behavior, but they too, like others from different cultures, want to show they are right for the job. Here is where moderation comes into play. A Chinese in this situation wants to strike a balance between talking too highly about one's ability (to do so would be arrogant)

and being so modest, so moderate, that one loses the job.

A Chinese job applicant will be careful to mention during the interview that the job will provide an opportunity to learn more and grow in experience. In other words, the applicant wants to show how he/she will gain from the company, rather than how the company will gain from him. Direct questions about salary and opportunities for advancement will not be normally posed by the applicant. Normally Chinese people would try to avoid such "bragging-like" words as "我的英語很流利" or "我的...很不錯", instead, they would be more likely to use phases such as, "...還可以" or state the facts, "我學了五年...,我會..."

Now recent changes in Chinese life have weakened these traditional concepts of personal moderation, especially among the youth, but they are still strong in Chinese society.

# 第九課聽力練習

## 第一部分：單句

請你們聽下面的句子。每個句子的意思是什麼？請在三個選擇中選出一句來。
Listen to the recorded statements. Circle the sentence from the three choices which is closest in meaning to the statement heard.

1.　　(a)甜的、鹹的糕點我都不喜歡。
　　　(b)我不喜歡甜的糕點。
　　　(c)我不喜歡鹹的糕點。

2.　　(a)經理還沒跟他面談就決定要僱他了。
　　　(b)經理覺得他的學歷、經驗都很不錯，想跟他做一次面談。
　　　(c)他的學歷、經驗使經理很滿意，所以面談後經理就決定僱他了。

3.　　(a)我以前在一家電腦公司工作過。
　　　(b)我現在在一家電腦公司工作。
　　　(c)我希望以後能到電腦公司去工作。

4.　　(a)這個人對自己的能力很有信心。
　　　(b)這個人又有能力，又有信心。
　　　(c)這個人做事我不放心，因為他的訓練還不夠。

5.　　(a)他對推銷產品很有經驗。
　　　(b)他沒有過推銷產品的經驗。
　　　(c)他對推銷產品很有興趣。

6.　　(a)這本字典對你沒有用。
　　　(b)這本字典能幫助你學習得更好。
　　　(c)你不需要這本字典。

7.　　(a)我是業務經理的秘書。
　　　(b)我多半負責發展出口業務。
　　　(c)我對發展出口業務很有興趣。

## 第二部分：短文

第一遍:請你們聽懂這篇短文的大意，然後看看下面這兩個句子說得對不對。

First Listening:  Listen to the recorded story.  Try to get a general idea of what it is about.  After you listen, decide whether these statements are true or false.

_____ 1.這個公司想找一位新秘書。
_____ 2.今天來參加面試的兩位小姐都很有經驗。

第二遍:請你們讀下面的問題，然後把這篇短文一段一段地再聽一次。聽完每一段後，請回答問題。

Second Listening:  Read the following questions.  Then listen to the story paragraph by paragraph and pay attention to details.  After you listen to each paragraph, answer the questions.

第一段：　　　1.楊小姐在這個公司做什麼工作？
　　　　　　　　　a)總經理　　　　　　b)秘書　　　　　　c)業務助理

　　　　　　　2.楊小姐為什麼要離開這個公司？
　　　　　　　　　a)因為工作環境不好　　　　b)因為薪水不夠高
　　　　　　　　　c)因為她結婚以後就要移民到加拿大去了

　　　　　　　3.我們要找的新秘書<u>不需要</u>什麼條件？
　　　　　　　　　a)大學畢業　　　　b)主修英文　　　　c)認真負責

第二段：　　　1.第一位來參加面試的小姐是一個什麼樣的人？
　　　　　　　　　a)主修英文　　　b)很有經驗　　　c)剛從大學畢業

　　　　　　　2.第一位小姐跟經理面談的時候怎麼樣？
　　　　　　　　　a)很緊張　　　　b)很有信心　　　c)很著急

第三段：　　　1.參加面試的第二位小姐，出國以前曾經做過什麼工作？
　　　　　　　　a)業務助理　　　b)秘書　　　c)業務代表

　　　　　　　2.第二位小姐在美國留學的時候，曾經在哪裡當過秘書？
　　　　　　　　a)圖書館　　　b)東亞系辦公室　　c)進出口公司

第三遍:請你們讀下面的問題，然後聽第三遍。聽完後，請回答問題。

Third Listening:  Read the following question.  Then listen to the story a third time.  After you listen, answer the question.

第一位小姐和第二位小姐在<u>學歷</u>和<u>工作經驗</u>方面有些什麼不同？

# 第九課　練習
## 辭彙；句型；語法

I.填入適當的詞語：

1. 負責：他＿＿＿＿（很）不負責；你應該＿＿＿＿這件事負責。/誰負責＿＿＿
　　　　＿＿＿＿＿＿＿＿＿＿＿＿＿？
2. 代表：＿＿＿＿＿＿代表；代表＿＿＿＿＿＿；明天開歡迎晚會我們請他
　　　　代表我們＿＿＿＿＿＿。
3. 能力：＿＿＿＿＿＿的能力；他的閱讀能力很＿＿＿＿。/這個人很＿＿＿能力。
4. 經驗：＿＿＿＿＿＿經驗；他的經驗＿＿＿＿＿＿＿。/在＿＿＿＿＿方面，
　　　　他很＿＿＿＿＿＿。
5. 興趣：他的興趣＿＿＿＿＿＿，但是對＿＿＿＿＿特別＿＿＿興趣。
6. 聯絡：你常＿＿＿＿他聯絡嗎？/明天我們＿＿＿＿電話聯絡吧。/我們已經
　　　　幾年＿＿＿＿聯絡了。
7. 方面：在＿＿＿＿方面；我對＿＿＿＿＿＿方面的業務不太熟悉。
8. 信心：我對＿＿＿＿＿＿（沒）有信心。/我在說中文方面的信心＿＿＿。
9. 發展：發展＿＿＿＿；＿＿＿＿（方面）的發展；發展＿＿＿＿＿很慢；
　　　　這個公司準備發展＿＿＿＿＿＿＿＿＿的業務。
10.訓練：訓練＿＿＿＿；＿＿＿＿的訓練；訓練了＿＿＿＿；訓練得＿＿＿＿

II.用"有"字詞組改寫下面的句子

我覺得我一定會找到工作。（信心）　＿＿＿＿＿＿＿＿＿＿＿＿＿＿＿＿

我覺得我不一定能找到工作。（信心）＿＿＿＿＿＿＿＿＿＿＿＿＿＿＿＿

看了這本書後我學中文容易多了。（幫助）＿＿＿＿＿＿＿＿＿＿＿＿＿＿

我看了這本書後沒學到什麼東西。（幫助）＿＿＿＿＿＿＿＿＿＿＿＿＿＿

我的朋友的能力很強。（能力）　　＿＿＿＿＿＿＿＿＿＿＿＿＿＿＿＿

我的朋友的能力有點兒差。（能力）＿＿＿＿＿＿＿＿＿＿＿＿＿＿＿＿

她知道不知道怎麼做業務助理？（經驗）＿＿＿＿＿＿＿＿＿＿＿＿＿＿

在業務方面她知道很多。（經驗）　＿＿＿＿＿＿＿＿＿＿＿＿＿＿＿＿

# 閱讀練習

I. 請看下面的短文。第一遍看懂大意；第二遍猜出或者查出不懂的詞。

## 第一次找工作

剛畢業的時候我很興奮，我想：啊，總算我<u>不用再</u>1看書、再考試了！總算我可以開始工作、不用再<u>靠</u>2父母了！於是我每天都在外面跑，到處找工作。可是沒有多久我就越來越沒有信心了，<u>甚至</u>3覺得<u>不如</u>4回學校<u>繼續</u>5看書考試去。原因是我面試了差不多五次了，每次開始時都好像很<u>有希望</u>6，可是到最後總是說我沒有工作經驗，所以不僱我。我越想越覺得不<u>服氣</u>7：有經驗的人就一定能力強，沒有經驗的人就一定能力差嗎？比如說，如果有兩個人一起來申請這個工作，<u>甲</u>8是一個有經驗的人，但是一個因為工作不好被<u>解僱</u>9了的人，而<u>乙</u>10是一個沒有經驗但是願意學的人，那麼你要甲還是要乙呢？所以我認為最重要的應該是看這個人願不願意學，有沒有發展的<u>潛力</u>11，而不是看他原來的經驗有多少。<u>失敗</u>12了幾次以後，我最後想出了一個主意。上星期面試時我對<u>僱主</u>13說：“您看能不能這樣：您先<u>試用</u>14我一個月；一個月後，如果你覺得我沒有能力做這個工作，那麼我會高高興興地離開這個公司。試用的時候你可以不給我薪水。” 僱主聽了這個話，覺得<u>有道理</u>15，<u>同意</u>16試試。我很高興他給了我這個機會。我想，<u>就是</u>17我一個月後不能留在這個公司工作，那麼我也算一個有工作經驗的人了，這次機會就<u>等於</u>18一次工作<u>實習</u>19和訓練吧。不過現在我有信心了：我相信我是有能力做好這個工作的。

<u>生詞表</u>（請查出空著的詞的意思）：

1.不用再... ＿＿＿＿＿＿＿＿＿＿＿  
2.靠 [kào]to depend on  
3.甚至 [shènzhì] even (go so far as to)  
4.不如 ＿＿＿＿＿＿＿＿＿＿＿  
5.繼續 [jìxù]to continue  
6.有希望 [yǒuxīwàng]to have great chance to... 
7.服氣 ＿＿＿＿＿＿＿＿＿＿＿  
8.甲 ＿＿＿＿＿＿＿＿＿＿＿  
9.解僱 [jiěgù]to fire (sb.)  
10.乙 ＿＿＿＿＿＿＿＿＿＿＿  

11.潛力 [qiánlì]potential  
12.失敗 [shībài]to fail; failure  
13.僱主 ＿＿＿＿＿＿＿＿＿＿＿  
14.試用 ＿＿＿＿＿＿＿＿＿＿＿  
15.有道理 [yǒu dàoli] to make sense  
16.同意 ＿＿＿＿＿＿＿＿＿＿＿  
17.就是...也... ＿＿＿＿＿＿＿＿＿＿＿  
18.等於 ＿＿＿＿＿＿＿＿＿＿＿  
19.實習 [shíxí]practice, internship

回答問題：下面説的對不對？如果不對，什麼地方不對？(寫出來)

1.他畢業的時候很興奮，因為他對自己找到工作很有信心。

2.他覺得上大學時看書考試很辛苦。

3.他上大學時跟父母借了很多錢。

4.他找了很長時間，都沒有找到合適的工作。

5.他上大學的時候沒有工作過，所以沒有什麼工作經驗。

6.面試他的幾個僱主都不願意僱沒有經驗的人。

7.他認為，有經驗的人不一定能力強，沒有經驗的人不見得能力差。

8.如果他自己是僱主，他會願意僱一個沒有經驗但願意學的人。

9.他最近找到了一個沒有薪水的工作，但是只能工作一個月。

10.他找這個工作主要是為了工作實習和經驗，他並不打算留在這個公司。

II.請看下面的廣告，然後寫出回答：

### 美商在台分公司徵才三名

大專或夜大學生，具英文讀寫
能力，對行政管理工作有興趣。
月薪二萬八加高額獎金。月入五
萬以上。每週上班五天，出國
旅遊、受訓練機會多。

### 回答問題

1.哪國公司？＿＿＿＿＿＿＿＿＿＿
2.學歷？＿＿＿＿＿＿＿＿＿＿＿＿
3.英文程度？＿＿＿＿＿＿＿＿＿＿
4.興趣？＿＿＿＿＿＿＿＿＿＿＿＿
5.月薪？＿＿＿＿＿＿＿＿＿＿＿＿
6.月收入？＿＿＿＿＿＿＿＿＿＿＿
7.有什麼機會？＿＿＿＿＿＿＿＿＿

# 口語練習

I.練習説下面的句子：

僱主：

能不能請你談談你的情況（工作經驗、想法）？
你有什麼工作經驗（特長 tècháng: expertise）？
你為什麼對這個工作感興趣？
請你回去等候通知。/我們過幾天會給你通知。

申請人：

我對這個工作很感興趣（很熟悉、很有經驗）。
我很想在這方面發展。
我在大學裡的主修是......
我會很快熟悉業務的。
我有信心做好這個工作。
我一定會努力工作的。
我很希望能得到這個工作。
我希望你們能給我一個機會試一試。
我能不能問一下月薪是多少？（底薪；年薪；起薪）
謝謝你們給我這個工作機會。
希望以後多多指點(zhǐdiǎn: advice, guidance)

II.情景會話：工作面試

請兩個人一組，選下面的一種工作面試。

1. 職務：北京一家大飯店經理助理；　　薪水：起薪2000元/月；有獎金(jiǎngjīn: bonus)

   工作時數：每天9小時；每星期六天；條件：大學畢業，中英文流利，熟悉電腦，

   有一年經驗，熱情，做事認真、負責

2. 職務：廣東一所中學英文老師；　　薪水：1000元/月起；學校給住房

   工作時數：每學期教兩門課；每星期20個課時

   條件：美國人，大學畢業學歷，有教英語的經驗，熱情，工作認真負責

# 寫作練習

1.<u>談看法</u>：如果你是僱主，你覺得你應該僱什麼樣的人？為什麼？

2.<u>談理想</u>：請你談談自己的工作興趣：你將來可能會想找什麼樣的工作？
喜歡什麼樣的工作環境？為什麼？

3.<u>比較</u>：下面的圖代表不同的工作。請選其中兩個，在下面這幾個方面作
一個比較：

- 要求什麼學歷、經驗？
- 收入怎麼樣？
- 工作辛苦嗎？

圖1.教師 teacher　　　　　　　　　　　圖2.秘書 secretary

圖3.工程師 [gōngchéngshī] engineer　　　圖4.律師 [lüshī] lawyer

圖5.醫生 [yīshēng] doctor　　　　　　　圖6.公司僱員 company employee

<u>用下面的句型做比較</u>：

在……方面，A比B……；　　　　　　A跟B在……方面差不多；

A在……方面跟B不同；　　　　　　在……方面，A不如B那麼……；

在……方面，A沒有B那麼……；　　跟A比起來，B……好得多／差得多

# 附錄
## APPENDICES

### A. 習字表
Character Writing Guides

### B. 句型和習慣用語
Sentence Patterns and Expressions Index

### C. 辭彙表
Vocabulary Glossary

# Appendix A

習字表（1—9課）

## Character Writing Guides (Lessons 1-9)

第一課單字表

| Regular Character | Simplified | Pronunciation Sample Word | Radical | Regular Character | Simplified | Pronunciation Sample Word | Radical |
|---|---|---|---|---|---|---|---|
| 奮 | 奋 | fèn 興奮 | 大 | 民 | | mín 人民 | 氏 |
| 準 | 准 | zhǔn 準備 | 水 / 氵 | 級 | 级 | jí 高級班 | 糸 / 纟 |
| 飛 | 飞 | fēi 飛機 | 飛 | 段 | | duàn 一段話 | 殳 |
| 票 | | piào 門票 | 示 / 礻 | 而 | | ér 而且 | 而 |
| 收 | | shōu 收拾 | 攴 / 攵 | 且 | | qiě 而且 | 一 |
| 拾 | | shí 收拾 | 手 / 扌 | 面 | | miàn 見面 | 面 |
| 部 | | bù 西部 | 邑 / 阝 | 種 | 种 | zhǒng 這種書 | 禾 / 禾 |
| 華 | 华 | Huá 華裔 | 艸 / 艹 | 傻 | | shǎ 傻樣子 | 人 / 亻 |
| 裔 | | yì 美裔 | 衣 / 衤 | 祝 | | zhù 祝你…. | 示 / 礻 |
| 移 | | yí 移民 | 禾 / 禾 | 順 | 顺 | shùn 順風 | 頁 |

| Regular Character | Simplified | Pronunciation Sample Word | Radical |
|---|---|---|---|
| 同 | | tóng<br>同學 | 口 |
| 達 | 达 | dá<br>到達 | 辵 / 辶 |
| 趕 | 赶 | gǎn<br>趕快 | 走 |
| 處 | 处 | chù<br>出口處 | 虍 |
| 向 | | xiàng<br>向前走 | 口 |
| 租 | | zū<br>租房子 | 禾 / 禾 |
| 突 | | tū<br>突然 | 穴 |
| 接 | | jiē<br>接朋友 | 手 / 扌 |
| 歡 | 欢 | huān<br>歡迎 | 欠 |
| 迎 | | yíng<br>歡迎 | 辵 / 辶 |

| Regular Character | Simplified | Pronunciation Sample Word | Radical |
|---|---|---|---|
| 室 | | shì<br>教室 | 宀 |
| 亞 | 亚 | Yǎ<br>亞可 | 二 |
| 辛 | | xīn<br>辛苦 | 辛 |
| 苦 | | kǔ<br>辛苦 | 艸 / 艹 |

# 第三課單字表

| Regular Character | Simplified | Pronunciation Sample Word | Radical | Regular Character | Simplified | Pronunciation Sample Word | Radical |
|---|---|---|---|---|---|---|---|
| 畢 | 毕 | bì 畢業 | 田 | 排 | | pái 安排 | 手 / 扌 |
| 業 | 业 | yè 畢業 | 木 / 朩 | 藉 | | jiè 藉機會 | 艸 / 艹 |
| 灣 | 湾 | wān 台灣 | 水 / 氵 | 戀 | 恋 | liàn 戀愛 | 心 / 忄 |
| 修 | | xiū 主修 | 人 / 亻 | 交 | | jiāo 交朋友 | 亠 |
| 濟 | 济 | jì 經濟 | 水 / 氵 | 隨 | 随 | suí 隨便 | 阜 / 左阝 |
| 熟 | | shóu 熟悉 | 火 / 灬 | 斷 | 断 | duàn 一刀兩斷 | 斤 |
| 悉 | | xī 熟悉 | 心 / 忄 | 研 | | yán 研究 | 石 |
| 況 | 况 | kuàng 情況 | 水 / 氵 | 究 | | jiū 研究 | 穴 |
| 閒 | 闲 | xián 管閒事 | 門 | 驚 | 惊 | jīng 大驚小怪 | 馬 |
| 幹 | 干 | gàn 能幹 | 干 | 互 | | hù 互相 | 二 |

# 第四課單字表

| Regular Character | Simplified | Pronunciation / Sample Word | Radical |
|---|---|---|---|
| 醫 | 医 | yī / 醫生 | 酉 |
| 環 | 环 | huán / 環境 | 玉 |
| 境 | | jìng / 環境 | 土 / 圡 |
| 感 | | gǎn / 感冒 | 心 / 忄 |
| 冒 | | mào / 感冒 | 冂 |
| 藥 | 药 | yào / 吃藥 | 艸 / 艹 |
| 反 | | fǎn / 反而 | 又 |
| 疼 | | téng / 頭疼 | 疒 |
| 務 | 务 | wù / 醫務室 | 力 |
| 檢 | 检 | jiǎn / 檢查 | 木 / 朩 |

| Regular Character | Simplified | Pronunciation / Sample Word | Radical |
|---|---|---|---|
| 查 | | chá / 檢查 | 木 / 朩 |
| 量 | | liáng / 量體溫 | 里 |
| 發 | 发 | fā / 發燒 | 癶 |
| 燒 | 烧 | shāo / 發燒 | 火 / 灬 |
| 度 | | dù / 溫度 | 广 |
| 呼 | | hū / 呼吸 | 口 |
| 吸 | | xī / 呼吸 | 口 |
| 麵 | 面 | miàn / 涼麵 | 麥 / 麦 |
| 衛 | 卫 | wèi / 衛生 | 行 |
| 鮮 | 鲜 | xiān / 新鮮 | 魚 |

| Regular Character | Simplified | Pronunciation Sample Word | Radical |
|---|---|---|---|
| 削 | | xiāo 削皮 | 刀／刂 |
| 證 | 证 | zhèng 證明 | 言 |
| 假 | | jià 請假 | 人／亻 |
| 偏 | | piān 偏偏 | 人／亻 |
| 厲 | 厉 | lì 厲害 | 厂 |
| 害 | | hài 厲害 | 宀 |

| Regular Character | Simplified | Pronunciation Sample Word | Radical |
|---|---|---|---|
| 加 | | jiā 加上 | 力 |
| 遲 | 迟 | chí 遲到 | 辵／辶 |
| 嚴 | 严 | yán 嚴格 | 口 |
| 格 | | gé 嚴格 | 木／木 |
| 視 | 视 | shì 重視 | 見 |
| 努 | | nǔ 努力 | 力 |
| 認 | 认 | rèn 認為 | 言 |
| 食 | | shí 食堂 | 食／食 |
| 規 | 规 | guī 規定 | 見 |
| 複 | 复 | fù 複習 | 衣／衤 |

| Regular Character | Simplified | Pronunciation Sample Word | Radical |
|---|---|---|---|
| 聊 | | liáo / 聊天 | 耳 |
| 流 | | liú / 流行 | 水／氵 |
| 曲 | | qǔ / 歌曲 | 曰 |
| 停 | | tíng / 停車 | 人／亻 |
| 並 | 并 | bìng / 並且 | 一 |
| 受 | | shòu / 難受 | 又 |
| 寂 | | jí / 寂寞 | 宀 |
| 寞 | | mò / 寂寞 | 宀 |
| 切 | | qiè / 一切 | 刀 |
| 儘 | 尽 | jìn / 儘快 | 人／亻 |

| Regular Character | Simplified | Pronunciation Sample Word | Radical |
|---|---|---|---|
| 緊 | 紧 | ﹣jǐn / 緊張 | 糸／纟 |
| 轉 | 转 | zhuǎn / 轉給他 | 車 |
| 態 | 态 | tài / 態度 | 心 |
| 度 | | dù / 態度 | 广 |

# 第六課單字表

| Regular Character | Simplified | Pronunciation / Sample Word | Radical |
|---|---|---|---|
| 喂 | | wéi/wèi / 喂,喂! | 口 |
| 盼 | | pàn / 盼望 | 目/四 |
| 數 | 数 | shǔ / 數日子 | 攴/攵 |
| 閉 | 闭 | bì / 閉眼睛 | 門 |
| 趁 | | chèn / 趁機會 | 走 |
| 撥 | 拨 | bō / 撥電話 | 手/扌 |
| 途 | | tú / 長途 | 辵/辶 |
| 般 | | bān / 一般 | 舟 |
| 該 | 该 | gāi / 應該 | 言 |
| 死 | | sǐ / 餓死了 | 歹 |

| Regular Character | Simplified | Pronunciation / Sample Word | Radical |
|---|---|---|---|
| 麻 | | má / 麻煩 | 麻 |
| 煩 | 烦 | fán / 麻煩 | 火/灬 |
| 通 | | tōng / 接通 | 辵/辶 |
| 留 | | liú / 留話 | 田 |
| 急 | | jí / 着急 | 心/忄 |
| 掛 | 挂 | guà / 掛斷 | 手/扌 |
| 傷 | 伤 | shāng / 傷心 | 人/亻 |
| | | | |
| | | | |
| | | | |

| Regular Character | Simplified | Pronunciation / Sample Word | Radical |
|---|---|---|---|
| 廣 | 广 | guǎng / 廣告 | 广 |
| 廳 | 厅 | tīng / 客廳 | 广 |
| 寓 | | yù / 公寓 | 宀 |
| 區 | 区 | qū / 地區 | 匚 |
| 整 | | zhěng / 整齊 | 攴 / 攵 |
| 齊 | 齐 | qí / 整齊 | 齊 |
| 套 | | tào / 一套書 | 大 |
| 式 | | shì / 中式傢俱 | 弋 |
| 使 | | shǐ / 使人高興 | 人 / 亻 |
| 浴 | | yù / 浴室 | 水 / 氵 |

| Regular Character | Simplified | Pronunciation / Sample Word | Radical |
|---|---|---|---|
| 滿 | 满 | mǎn / 滿意 | 水 / 氵 |
| 郵 | 邮 | yóu / 郵局 | 邑 / 右阝 |
| 局 | | jú / 郵局 | 尸 |
| 銀 | 银 | yín / 銀行 | 金 / 釒 |
| 園 | 园 | yuán / 公園 | 囗 |
| 煙 | 烟 | yān / 吸煙 | 火 / 灬 |
| 括 | | kuò / 包括 | 手 / 扌 |
| 內 | | nèi / 在內 | 入 |
| 費 | 费 | fèi / 水電費 | 貝 |
| 商 | | shāng / 商量 | 口 |

# 第八課單字表

| Regular Character | Simplified | Pronunciation Sample Word | Radical | Regular Character | Simplified | Pronunciation Sample Word | Radical |
|---|---|---|---|---|---|---|---|
| 樂 | 乐 | lè<br>樂一樂 | 木／木 | 餅 | 饼 | bǐng<br>月餅 | 食／食 |
| 節 | 节 | jié<br>中秋節 | 竹／灬 | 減 | 减 | jiǎn<br>減肥 | 水／氵 |
| 參 | 参 | cān<br>參加 | 厶 | 肥 | | féi<br>減肥 | 肉／月 |
| 舞 | | wǔ<br>跳舞 | 舛 | 甜 | | tián<br>甜味 | 甘 |
| 系 | | xì<br>中文系 | 系／糸 | 鹹 | 咸 | xián<br>鹹味 | 鹵 |
| 邀 | | yāo<br>邀請 | 辵／辶 | 推 | | tuī<br>推薦 | 手／扌 |
| 品 | | pǐn<br>食品 | 口 | 薦 | 荐 | jiàn<br>推薦 | 艸／艹 |
| 售 | | shòu<br>售貨員 | 口 | 顧 | 顾 | gù<br>顧客 | 頁 |
| 貨 | 货 | huò<br>售貨員 | 貝 | 油 | | yóu<br>奶油 | 水／氵 |
| 員 | 员 | yuán<br>售貨員 | 口 | 糕 | | gāo<br>糕點 | 米 |

| Regular Character | Simplified | Pronunciation / Sample Word | Radical |
|---|---|---|---|
| 盒 | | hé / 盒子 | 皿 |
| 裝 | 装 | zhuāng / 包裝 | 衣 / 衤 |
| 葡 | | pú / 葡萄 | 艸 / 艹 |
| 萄 | | táo / 葡萄 | 艸 / 艹 |
| 醉 | | zuì / 喝醉 | 酉 |
| 啤 | | pí / 啤酒 | 口 |
| 角 | | jiǎo / 五角錢 | 角 |
| 鬧 | 闹 | nào / 熱鬧 | 鬥 |
| 鬆 | 松 | sōng / 輕鬆 | 髟 |
| 聚 | | jù / 聚會 | 耳 |

| Regular Character | Simplified | Pronunciation / Sample Word | Radical |
|---|---|---|---|
| 僱 | 雇 | gù / 僱用 | 人 / 亻 |
| 頁 | 负 | fù / 頁責 | 貝 |
| 責 | 责 | zé / 頁責 | 貝 |
| 專 | 专 | zhuān / 大專 | 寸 |
| 強 | 强 | qiáng / 能力強 | 弓 |
| 驗 | 验 | yàn / 經驗 | 馬 |
| 薪 | | xīn / 薪水 | 艸 / 艹 |
| 趣 | | qù / 興趣 | 走 |
| 聯 | 联 | lián / 聯絡 | 耳 |
| 絡 | 络 | luò / 聯絡 | 糸 / 纟 |

| Regular Character | Simplified | Pronunciation Sample Word | Radical |
|---|---|---|---|
| 需 | | xū<br>需要 | 雨 |
| 閱 | 阅 | yuè<br>閱讀 | 門 |
| 稍 | | shāo<br>稍低 | 禾 |
| 微 | | wēi<br>稍微 | 彳 |
| 術 | 术 | shù<br>術語 | 行 |
| 曾 | | céng<br>曾經 | 日 |
| 產 | 产 | chǎn<br>產品 | 生 |
| 銷 | 销 | xiāo<br>推銷 | 金／釒 |
| 展 | | zhǎn<br>發展 | 尸 |
| 職 | 职 | zhí<br>職務 | 耳 |

# Appendix B
# 句型和習慣用語（1—9課）
## Sentence Patterns and Expressions Index (Lessons 1-9)

Note: This list goes by the alphabetical order of the first character. In the rare occasion when no character is found in the pattern or expression, alphabetical order of the first English word is followed. Lesson number is listed at the end of each pattern/expression.

包括......(在內)，......( Including..., ... [totals] ...; include .... )  7
　　包括我在內，這裡一共有二十六個人。Including me, there are twenty-six people here.
　　明天的考試包括這一課的生字（在內）。Tomorrow's test will cover the new words of this lesson.

不但 ......,而且（也）......(not only ... but also...)  4
　　他不但（不）熟悉美國的情況，而且也（不）熟悉中國的情況。
　　He is not only familiar with the goings-on in the U.S., but also with those in China.

不管......，都 V......( no matter what/who/when/where/how... )  3
　　不管我說什麼，他都不聽。No matter what I say, he just won't listen.

不是A,就是B (It is either A or B; If it's not A, it must be B)  6
　　大為的電話真不好打，不是佔線，就是沒人接。
　　It's hard to reach David by phone. Either the line is busy or no one answers the phone.

(Clause) +（不要緊/很重要/很好/不好）(It is [unimportant / important /good/bad,etc.] to/
　　that...)  5
　　學得慢不要緊，可是一定要努力。It's OK if you are slow (in studying), but you must study hard.
　　房間夠不夠大很重要。Whether the room is large enough is very important.
　　晚上一個人在街上走不好。It's not good to walk by oneself in the street late at night.

不知道......怎麼樣？( I wonder what...is like？)  7
　　不知道這裡的環境怎麼樣？I wonder what the environment here is like.

不知道怎麼搞的，......(who knows how it happened...;  I've no idea ...; somehow... )  4
　　不知道怎麼搞的，我這幾天總是睡不好覺。I don't know why these days I haven't been sleeping well.

曾經 V 過 ( ever did sth. in the past )  9
　　我曾經在中國待過一段時間。  I once stayed in China for a period of time.

趁......V（taking advantage of... to do...）6

趁我父母不在家，我趕快給他打了個電話。

Taking advantage of my parents' not being home, I hurriedly gave him a call.

趁早V（do sth. as early as possible / while one can / before it's too late）6

如果你不愛他，就趁早跟他吹了吧。

If you don't love him, why don't you break up with him before it's too late.

到底（what/who/when/where/how in the world......?）2

這到底是怎麼回事？ What exactly is going on?

他到底是誰？ Who on earth is he?/ Who exactly is he?

Adj. / V 得......（Sb. / sth. ... so ...that...）1

我高興得說不出話來。 I was so happy that I was speechless.

(Clause), V/Adj. 得 sb.(+ result/extent )(...so much so that it causes/caused...) 5

他老在宿舍裡唱歌，唱得我頭大。

He always sings in the dorm and that drives me crazy.

......得......才行(Sb. has got to do ...before...) 4

你得適應這裡的條件才行。You've got to get adjusted to the conditions here.

等......再V......（wait until ... and then...）6

等我把功課復習完了再跟你出去看電影。

After I finish reviewing my lessons, I'll go to the movies with you.

都怪......（It's all sb's fault that...; Sb. is to blame）8

你一喝酒就醉，都怪你不會克制自己。You get drunk every time you drink and you are the one to blame because you don't know how to control yourself.

對......感/有興趣（be interested in...; to take interest in....）9

我對這個工作很感興趣。I am very interested in this job.

對......來說，......（As far as Sb. is concerned...; For Sb. ...）1

這一次分別，對他們兩個人來說都有一點兒不容易。

It is not easy at all for the two of them to part this time.

該V了（It's time to......）3

你已經三十多歲了，該結婚了。

You're already over thirty. It's time for you to get married!

好(不)容易才 V ( had great difficulty before finally... ) 8

我找了幾個月，好(不)容易才找到一個滿意的公寓。

I looked for an apartment for months [and had a hard time] before I finally found a satisfactory one.


...... , 好在 ...... ( ..., fortunately, ... ) 5

我前幾天忙死了，好在他來了，幫了我不少忙。

I was extremely busy a few days ago. Fortunately he came and helped me a great deal.


...... , 加上 ...... , 結果 ...... ( ..., plus... then,[sth. happened]) 5

他到了新地方，身體不適應，加上又喜歡吃生冷的東西，結果生了一次病。

He had just come to a new place and wasn't accustomed to the new environment.  Moreover, he likes to eat raw or cold food; then, he got sick.


藉 ...機會 V ( take the opportunity to ...) 3

他想藉留學中國的機會好好地熟悉一下中國的情況。

He wants to take the opportunity of studying abroad in China to get familiar with China.


Sb. ...(QW-form) 就 ...(QW-form)  ( sb. does whatever sb. wants to ... ) 8

誰想吃什麼就吃什麼吧。  Anyone can eat whatever he/she wants.


就 V 好了 ( Why don't you just...... ) 8

我叫李大為，你就叫我大為好了。 My name is Li Dawei. Why don't you just call me Dawei.


(Location)就是 (Place)   (Right at [location] is [place] / You'll find [place] right at [location] ) 7

學校前頭就是一條大馬路。 A broad street is right in front of the school.

街對面就是銀行。 The bank is right across the street.


就 ...... , 也...... ( even if..., sb/sth.... ) 4

你就是給他錢，他也不會願意做這件事的。 He won't do this even if you give him money.


看上去 ......(...looks/looked like...) 7

她看上去只有五十多歲。  She looks like she is only in her fifties.


看樣子 ......(It seems/looks like... ) 2

看樣子他不會來了。  It doesn't look like he is coming./It looks like he is not coming.


V 來 V 去 , 就是 (neg.)... ( Sb. kept doing sth. but just couldn't / didn't... ) 2

我想來想去，就是想不出一個好法子來。

I thought about it over and over, but I just couldn't come up with a good idea.

VP了 (+ comment) ( If/Once sb. [does/has done...], then [sth. will happen]) 5

你得早一點到食堂去，去晚了就買不到飯了。
You'd better go to the cafeteria earlier. If you go there late you won't be able to buy food.

Location/Time + Locomotive Verb + indef. performer (indef. Performer + Locomotive Verb + [Location/Time]) 2

前面走過來幾個人。 A few people were approaching from the distance ahead.

麻煩你 V...。/麻煩你 V......好嗎？ (Please [do me a favor and].../ Could you please [do...]?) 6

麻煩你請他接一下電話好嗎？ Could you tell him to answer the phone please?

忙 着......( sb.is/was busy doing... [during/when...]) 7

這幾天她正在忙着找房子。 She is busy looking for a house these days.

没(duration of time)就 V 了 ( sb.\ sth. .... in less than [time] ) 4

他到了美國以後，没兩天就生病了。 He got sick just a few days after he arrived in the U.S.

你看(說、覺得)(Sb.) V...好？ (What would you suggest?/What [where, etc.] do you think [sb.] should ...?) 8

我想買一點兒吃的東西，你看（我）買什麼好？ I'd like to buy some food. What do you think/suggest/recommend I should buy?

.....你看(說，覺得，認為)怎麼樣？ ( ......What do you think？) 9

我們今天晚上出去吃飯，你看怎麼樣？ Let's eat out tonight. What do you think？

.....，其中......（ ......, among whom/which; of which ... ） 2

我有二十本書，其中有五本中文書。 I have twenty books, five of which are Chinese books.

...... 使 ...... (Sb. / Sth. makes / made sb. / sth. ....) 7

他的話使我很高興。 His words made me happy./His words pleased me.

Sb.是第一次......（ It is sb's first time......）2

你是第一次來紐約嗎？ Is this your first time in New York?

受... ；受到... （歡迎，重視，喜愛...）(...received [popularity, attention, favor, etc.]) 8

這個飯館受到很多顧客歡迎。 /這個飯館很受顧客歡迎。
This restaurant is favored by many customers.

雖然......，但是總比......多了（ Although...yet it's much more... than...）5

雖然這個房子不夠大，可是總比宿舍好多了。
Although this house is not big enough, it is much better than the dormitory.

Subject 爲 (sb. / sth)...... （而）... (Subject is / does... for the sake of/because of/on behalf of ...) 3
他一天到晚爲家事而忙得團團轉。
Because of his housework, he is always so busy that he doesnüt know he is coming or going.

爲了......，...... ( in order to; for the sake of)  1
爲了把中文說好，大爲要到北京去學習。
David will go to Beijing to study in order to speak Chinese well.

一邊......，一邊...... ( Sb. does/did one thing while doing another )  5
他一邊看書，一邊聽流行歌曲。He listened to hit/popular songs while reading.

一是......，二是...... ( for one thing..., for another... )  3
我没有去找他，一是我太忙，二是我不知道他住在哪裡。
I didnüt go to see him, because for one I was too busy, and for another, I didn't know where he lives.

.....，於是 (sb.) 就 V 了...... (..., so/thereupon sb. did sth. [as an immediate reaction])  9
那個電腦很好用，而且也不貴，於是我就買了。
That computer is user-friendly and it's not expensive either, so I bought it.

...再...也没有了/不過了  ( Sth. couldn't be better / worse, etc. ... )  3
這個人又聰明，長得又帥，對你再合適也没有了。
This man is both smart and handsome.  He is the perfect one for you/No one could be more suitable.

再過 time expression，就 V. ...了  (Sb./sth. will [...] in + [time])  1
再過幾天就是我妹妹的生日了。It will be my younger sister's birthday in a few days.

早不......晚不......，偏偏在...的時候V (Sb. does/did sth. at the worst time)  4
他早不來晚不來，偏偏在我要睡覺了的時候來了！(真要命！) He didn't come at a good time but chose to come just when I was about to go to sleep! Damn it!

Location +V 着+ sb./ sth. (There at [place] [verb] sth./sb.)  2
門上貼着一張字條。 On the door is attached a note.

V1 着V2 (Sb. is/has ....[accompaniment or means] while doing sth. )  4
他喜歡開着窗戶睡覺。He likes to sleep with the window open.
你別看着報紙吃飯。Do not eat your meal and read papers at the same time.

V 着V 着, V/Adj.起(O)來 (While..., ...started to ...)  4
這几天我老咳嗽。咳着咳着，頭也疼起來了。
These few days I've coughed all the time. As I coughed, my head began to hurt.

(time expression)(以)來......  (during/over the past [days/months,etc.],...）  1
這一個月(以)來，我看了不少書。 I have read quite a few books during the past month.


這(time expression)(以)來， Sb.都在 V... ( Sb. has been doing sth. for the past...）  1
這一個月來，他都在作出國準備。
He has been making preparations for going abroad for the past month.


只要......（就）......(as long as..., then...; ... provided that...)  7
只要你有錢，你就可以住很漂亮的房子。
You can live in a beautiful house as long as you have money.


...主要是......( mainly...; primarily...）  9
我們公司想找的業務代表主要是用英文。
The sales representative that our company is looking for will primarily speak and write in English.


自從......(point of time)以後，就 ... ...了( Ever since..., ....）  6
他自從結婚以後，就沒再給我打過電話了。 He hasn't called me since he got married.


A 總比 B Adj. 多了 (A is at least much more [adj.] than B.)  4
打電話總比寫信快多了。 Making a phone call is at least much faster than writing a letter.


左 V 右 V ，都(neg.)....../總算 (pos.)......了(kept doing sth, but still.../and finally...)  6
我左盼右盼都盼不來他的信。 I kept hoping to get letters from him, but I just never got any.
我左等右等都等不到他的電話。/我左等右等，總算等到了他的電話了。
I waited and waited; his phone call finally came.

# Appendix C
# 辭彙表
## Vocabulary Glossary (Lessons 1-9)

**A:**

| | | |
|---|---|---|
| ài shàng | 愛上/爱上 | RV to fall in love with  5 |
| àn | 按 | V to press; push down, depress  6 |
| àn | 按 | CV according to  7 |
| ānjìng | 安靜/安静 | ADJ quiet (安安靜靜地, quietly)  5 |
| ānpái | 安排 | V/N to arrange, schedule;  arrangement  3 |
| ānquán | 安全 | ADJ safe, secure  7 |
| ànshí | 按時/按时 | CV-O on time, [do...] according to scheduled time 7 |

**B:**

| | | |
|---|---|---|
| bàngōngshì | 辦公室/办公室 | N office, workplace  2 |
| bāngzhù | 幫助/帮助 | V/N to assist, help;  assistance  1 |
| bǎochí | 保持 | V to keep (clean, etc.), to maintain  7 |
| bāokuò | 包括 | V to include, contain  7 |
| bāokuò...zài nèi | 包括...在内 | VP including, with......included  7 |
| bāozhuāng | 包裝/包装 | V to pack, packaging  8 |
| bāozi | 包子 | N steamed stuffed bun (肉包子, bun stuffed with meat)  4 |
| bì(shang) | 閉(上)/闭(上) | RV to close (eyes, mouth, etc.)  6 |
| biǎo | 表 | N chart, table, list, form  9 |
| bǐfāngshuō | 比方說/比方说 | PH for example  5 |
| bǐng | 餅/饼 | N cake, pie, cookie  8 |
| bìng | 病 | N/V disease, ailment; to be sick  4 |
| bìngqiě | 並且 | MA moreover, and, and also (syn. ěrqiě, 而且）  5 |
| bìyè | 畢業/毕业 | VO/N to graduate; graduation  3 |
| bō | 撥/拨 | V to dial (the telephone), set/adjust (a watch, dial, etc.)  6 |
| bómǔ | 伯母 | N wife of father's elder brother; aunt  3 |
| bù | -部 | BF area, region (as PW Suffix)  1 |
| (yào)bùrán | (要)不然 | MA otherwise  5 |
| búdàn...érqiě | 不但...而且 | MA not only..., but also...  4 |
| bùguǎn | 不管 | MA no matter, regardless  3 |

| búyàode | 不見得/不见得 | MA [colloq.] not necessarily  5 |
|---|---|---|

**C:**

| cānjiā | 參加/参加 | V to participate, join  8 |
|---|---|---|
| céngjīng | 曾經/曾经 | A (did/was) once, ever  9 |
| chá | 查 | V to check, check over; look up (name, phone number, etc.)  6 |
| chà | 差 | ADJ poor (in quality, ability)  9 |
| chángtú | 長途/长途 | N long distance; long distance phone call  6 |
| chǎnpǐn | 產品/产品 | N product  9 |
| chèn | 趁 | CV take advantage of (a favorable situation)  6 |
| chéng | 成 | V to turn into, become  1 |
| chènzǎo | 趁早 | A (do) while you can (see *Patterns*)  6 |
| chídào | 遲到/迟到 | V to arrive late (for class, meeting)  5 |
| chī yào | 吃藥/吃药 | VO to take medicine (orally); (藥, medicine, remedy)  4 |
| chū | 出 | V to contribute, chip in (idea, money, etc.)  6 |
| chúfáng | 廚房/厨房 | N kitchen  7 |
| chuī le | 吹了 | IE [colloq.] (relationship)  broken up/split; (of a plan) failed/fell through  3 |
| chūkǒu | 出口 | V/N to export; export  9 |
| chūkǒuchù | 出口處/出口处 | N exit (出口 N exit; -處 -place, Noun-Suffix)  2 |
| chūzū | 出租 | V lease out; leased.  2 |
| chūzūchē | 出租車/出租车 | N taxi ('Taxi' is 計程車 [jìchéngchē] in Taiwan)  2 |

**D:**

| dá | 打 | M a dozen (note tone!)  8 |
|---|---|---|
| dāi | 待 | V to stay (at a place or for a time)  3 |
| dàibiǎo | 代表 | V/N to represent; representative  9 |
| dàngāo | 蛋糕 | N layer cake; cake  8 |
| dāngshí | 當時/当时 | TW at that time, then, at that very moment  1 |
| dàochù | 到處/到处 | PW everywhere  4 |
| dàodǐ | 到底 | MA after all  2 |
| dàodá | 到達/到达 | V/N to reach, arrive; arrival  2 |
| dàoshì | 倒(是) | A actually, on the other hand  8 |
| dǎ pēntì | 打噴嚔/打喷嚔 | VO to sneeze  4 |
| dǎsǎo | 打掃/打扫 | V. to clean (by mopping or sweeping)  7 |
| dàzhuān | 大專/大专 | N university & professional school  (abbr. of 大學 and 專科學校/专科学校 zhuānkē xuéxiào)  9 |
| dìdiǎn | 地點/地点 | N location, place (of an event)  8 |

| | | | |
|---|---|---|---|
| dīng | 叮 | (sound simulation of a phone ring/bell) 6 | |
| dìngjīn | 定金 | N deposit ( money paid in advance) 7 | |
| dìqū | 地區/地区 | PW area, region 7 | |
| dìzhǐ | 地址 | N address 5 | |
| Dōngyà | 東亞/东亚 | PW East Asia 3 | |
| dù | 度 | M degree (of temperature, angle, etc.) 4 | |
| duàn | 段 | M section, part 1 | |
| duìfāng | 對方/对方 | N the other party 6 | |
| duìxiàng | 對象/对象 | N (marriage) prospect; target, object 3 | |

**E:**

| | | |
|---|---|---|
| érqiě | 而且 | MA moreover, and also 1 |

**F:**

| | | |
|---|---|---|
| fángdōng | 房東/房东 | N landlord (of a rented house or building) 7 |
| fángkè | 房客 | N tenant 7 |
| fāngmiàn | 方面 | N aspect, area 9 |
| fàng//xīn | 放心 | VO/SV to rest assured, feel relieved 1 |
| fángzū | 房租 | N rent (for a house or room) 7 |
| fāpiào | 發票/发票 | N (sales) receipt 8 |
| fā//shāo | 發燒/发烧 | VO to have a fever 4 |
| fāxiàn | 發現/发现 | V/N to discover, find; discovery, finding 5 |
| fāzhǎn | 發展/发展 | V/N to develop; development 9 |
| fèi | 費/费 | N fee 7 |
| fēijī | 飛機/飞机 | N airplane 1 |
| fēnbié | 分別 | V/N/A to separate; separation; separately, respectively 1 |
| fēnjī | 分機/分机 | N (of phone system) extension 6 |
| fùxí | 複習/复习 | V/N to review (lessons); review 5 |
| fùzé | 負責/负责 | V be responsible (for), in charge of 9 |

**G:**

| | | |
|---|---|---|
| gāisǐ | 該死/该死 | IE [colloq.] damn (lit. "deserve death") 6 |
| gǎn | 敢 | AV to dare to 2 |
| gānbābā | 乾巴巴/干巴巴 | ADJ dry and dull 5 |
| gānjìng | 乾淨/干净 | ADJ be clean (洗乾淨,RV wash clean) 4 |
| gǎnkuài | 趕快/赶快 | A hurriedly, quickly 2 |

| gǎnmào | 感冒 | N/V flu, cold; to have a cold/flu  4 |
|---|---|---|
| gǎnqíng | 感情 | N emotion, feeling  5 |
| gǎn xìngqù | 感興趣/感兴趣 | VP be interested  9 |
| gàobié | 告別 | VO/N to bid farewell, say goodbye; farewell  1 |
| gāodiǎn | 糕點/糕点 | N pastry  8 |
| gāojí | 高級/高级 | ADJ high level/rank, ad-vanced, advanced level  1 |
| gāoyǎ | 高雅 | ADJ elegant  2 |
| gēn | 跟 | V to follow  5 |
| gēqǔ | 歌曲 | N song  5 |
| gōngkè | 功課/功课 | N course work, homework assignment  5 |
| gōngsī | 公司 | N company  9 |
| gōngyù | 公寓 | N apartment; apartment building  7 |
| gōngyuán | 公園/公园 | N park  7 |
| guà | 掛/挂 | V. hang; hang up (a phone); to ring off (sb. On the phone)  6 |
| guǎi | 拐 | V to make a turn (in direction)  7 |
| guàibude | 怪不得 | IE no wonder... (= to 難怪/难怪)  4 |
| guǎn | 管 | V to manage, take care [of a matter], in charge of  3 |
| guǎnggào | 廣告/广告 | N advertisement  7 |
| guǎn xiánshì | 管閒事/管闲事 | VP to butt into other people's business  3 |
| guīdìng | 規定/规定 | V/N to make it a rule that; rule, regulation  5 |
| gùkè | 顧客/顾客 | N customer, client  8 |
| guò | 過/过 | V to observe (a holiday, birthday, etc.)  8 |
| guò//jié | 過節/过节 | VO to observe the holiday  8 |
| -guòletóu | -過了頭/-过了头 | VP to overdo...; have overdone -睡過了頭 oversleep  5 |
| guòqù | 過去/过去 | TW in the past, formerly  9 |
| guǒrén | 果仁 | N nuts  8 |
| gùyòng | 僱(用)/雇(用) | V to hire (for employment)  9 |

## H:

| hāhā | 哈哈 | ON Ha, ha!  1 |
|---|---|---|
| hái kěyǐ | 還可以/还可以 | IE so-so, passable  2 |
| hǎo... | 好... | A [for emphasis] so..., terribly, awfully  6 |
| hàomǎ | 號碼/号码 | N number (room, phone, etc.); code  6 |
| hǎoxiào | 好笑 | ADJ be funny, amusing  1 |
| hǎozài | 好在 | MA [colloq.] fortunately, luckily  5 |
| hépíng | 和平 | ADJ/N peaceful; peace  5 |

| | | | |
|---|---|---|---|
| hézhuāng(de) | 盒裝(的)/盒装(的) | box-packed; boxed  8 | |
| hézi | 盒 | N box  8 | |
| huánjìng | 環境/环境 | N environment  4 | |
| huānyíng | 歡迎/欢迎 | V/N to welcome; welcome  2 | |
| Huáyì | 華裔/华裔 | N citizen of Chinese origin  1 | |
| huì | 會/会 | AV will/would, may/might, be likely  1 | |
| huì | 會/会 | N meeting, conference, party  8 | |
| huòzhě | 或者 | CONJ or (as in either...or...)  4 | |
| hùzhào | 護照/护照 | N passport  1 | |

## J:

| | | | |
|---|---|---|---|
| jí | -級/-级 | BF level, rank  1 | |
| jiājù | 傢具/家具 | N furniture  7 | |
| jiǎn | 減/减 | V to reduce, deduct, minus  8 | |
| jiǎnchá | 檢查/检查 | V/N to examine, inspect; checkup, inspection  4 | |
| jiǎnféi | 減肥/减肥 | VO to go on diet ("reduce fat")  8 | |
| jiàn//miàn | 見面/见面 | VO to meet (someone), see  1 | |
| jiāo | 交 | V to submit, turn in; pay (rent, etc.)  7 | |
| jiāo péngyou | 交朋友 | VP to make friends  3 | |
| jiāshàng | 加上 | MA/V plus the fact that. in addition; to add  5 | |
| jiē | 接 | V to pick up/meet (sb. at a station, airport, etc.); to receive (mail, phone call, etc.)  2 | |
| jiē | 接 | V to connect; to answer (phone)  6 | |
| jié | 節/节 | BF holiday, festival  8 | |
| jiè | 藉/借 | V by means of, take   (opportunity/ advantage to do sth.)  3 | |
| jiéguǒ | 結果/结果 | MA/N consequently, end up being...; result  4 | |
| jīhuì | 機會/机会 | N chance, opportunity  3 | |
| jiéhūn | 結婚/结婚 | VO to get married, to marry  3 | |
| jiěkāi | 解開/解开 | V to untie, unfasten  4 | |
| jǐnkuài | 儘快/尽快 | A as soon as possible, soon  5 | |
| jièkǒu | 藉口/借口 | N an excuse, a pretext  6 | |
| jiēxiànyuán | 接線員/接线员 | N (phone) operator  6 | |
| jiēzhe | 接着 | MA subsequently, then, immediately, next  7 | |
| -jīn | -金 | BF (lit. "gold") money, currency, a fund (used as N-Suf.)   7 | |
| jīngjì | 經濟/经济 | ADJ/N economical; economics, economy  3 | |
| jīnglǐ | 經理/经理 | N (business) manager (see notes)  9 | |

| | | | |
|---|---|---|---|
| jīngyàn | 經驗/经验 | N experience  9 | |
| jìnkǒu | 進口/进口 | V/N to import; import  9 | |
| jǐnzhāng | 緊張/紧张 | ADJ nervous, tense  9 | |
| jìmò | 寂寞 | ADJ lonely  5 | |
| jùhuì | 聚會/聚会 | V/N to get together; get-together, assembly, party  8 | |

**K:**

| | | |
|---|---|---|
| kāi | 開/开 | V to make out (a list, prescription, check)  4 |
| kànshàngqu | 看上去 | VP to look (young, tired, etc.)  7 |
| ké | 咳 | V cough  4 |
| Kěkǒu Kělè | 可口可樂/可口可乐 | N (transliteration of) Coca Cola  8 |
| késou | 咳嗽 | V/N to cough; cough  4 |
| kètīng | 客廳/客厅 | N living-room, parlor  7 |
| kèzhì | 克制 | V/N restrain, suppress; restraint, suppression  2 |
| kǒuyǔ | 口語/口语 | N spoken language  1 |
| kòuzi | 扣子 | N (clothes) button  4 |

**L:**

| | | |
|---|---|---|
| lè | 樂/乐 | V to have fun, amuse oneself  8 |
| lí | 離/离 | CV (distance) from (in space/time)  2 |
| lián | 連/连 | CV including, with......included  4 |
| liàn'ài | 戀愛/恋爱 | V/N be in love; romantic love  3 |
| liáng | 量 | V to measure (temperature, length, etc.)  4 |
| liánluò | 聯絡/联络 | V/N to get in touch; contact (between people)  9 |
| liáotiān | 聊天 | VO to chat  5 |
| Lǐ Dàwéi | 李大爲/李大为 | N (Chinese name of) David Leigh  1 |
| lìhai | 厲害/厉害 | ADJ severe  4 |
| lìngwài | 另外 | MA in addition, besides  4 |
| Lín Hóng | 林紅/林红 | N (name of a person)  2 |
| lìqi | 力氣/力气 | N. physical strength  4 |
| liú | 留 | V to leave (sth. for sb.) |
| liú huà | 留話/留话 | VP to leave a (verbal) message  6 |
| liúlì | 流利 | ADJ fluent  9 |
| liúxíng | 流行 | ADJ popular (song, fashion, etc.)  5 |
| liúxué | 留學/留学 | VO to study abroad  1 |
| lǚlìbiǎo | 履歷表/履历表 | N resume, curriculum vitae  9 |

| luōsuo | 囉嗦/啰嗦 | ADJ [of a person] repetitious and fussy  7 |
| lùyīnjī | 錄音機/录音机 | N tape recorder (錄音, V/N to make a tape recording; recording, tape)  5 |

## M:

| ma | 嘛 | p (Particle suggesting obviousness)  4 |
| máfan | 麻煩/麻烦 | V/N/SV to trouble; (put sb. to some) trouble; annoyance; troublesome  6 |
| Mǎlì | 瑪麗/玛丽 | N (transliteration of) Mary, Marie  8 |
| mǎlù | 馬路/马路 | N boulevard, avenue  7 |
| mǎnyì | 滿意/满意 | ADJ satisfied, content, happy with  7 |
| miàn | 面 | N side  2 |
| miàn | 麵/面 | N noodles; flour, dough  4 |
| miànshì | 面試/面试 | V/N to have a (job) interview; (job) interview 9 |
| miàntán | 面談/面谈 | V/N to talk face-to-face; face-to-face talk  9 |
| míngmíng | 明明 | A clearly, obviously  2 |
| mìshū | 秘書/秘书 | N secretary  9 |

## N:

| nǎiyóu | 奶油 | N butter, cream  8 |
| nánshòu | 難受/难受 | ADJ sad, unbearable, intolerable  4 |
| nénggàn | 能幹/能干 | ADJ capable, able  3 |
| nénglì | 能力 | N ability, capability  (abbr. As 力 in compounds)  9 |
| niàn | 唸/念 | V to read aloud, chant (poem, etc.)  5 |
| nǔlì | 努力 | V to strive, work hard (to achieve sth.)  5 |

## P:

| páizi | 牌子 | N sign; brand (of a product)  2 |
| pànwàng | 盼望 | V/N to look forward to; expectation  6 |
| pí | 皮 | N skin; leather  4 |
| piānpiān | 偏偏 | MA  4 |
| piào | 票 | N ticket  1 |
| píjiǔ | 啤酒 | N beer  8 |
| -pǐn | -品 | BF -stuff, item ( Noun-Suffix)  8 |
| pútao | 葡萄 | N grapes  8 |

## Q:

| qì | 氣/气 | N air, gas, vapor  4 |
| qiáng | 強/强 | ADJ strong, powerful  9 |

| | | |
|---|---|---|
| qiānzhèng | 簽證/签证 | N visa  1 |
| qiǎokelì: | 巧克力 | N (transliteration of) chocolate  8 |
| Qīngdǎo | 青島/青岛 | N (name of a Chinese city in Shandong, famous for its beer)  8 |
| qǐngjià | 請假/请假 | VO to ask for a leave of absence  4 |
| qíngkuàng | 情況/情况 | N situation, condition, status  3 |
| qīngsōng | 輕鬆/轻松 | ADJ light-hearted, relaxed, easy  8 |
| qīnqi | 親戚/亲戚 | N relatives (of extended family)  1 |
| qíshí | 其實/其实 | MA actually, as a matter of fact  6 |
| qìshuǐ | 汽水 | N soda (carbonated beverage)  8 |
| qízhōng | 其中 | PW among them; in which  2 |

## R:

| | | |
|---|---|---|
| rènao | 熱鬧/热闹 | ADJ (atmosphere) festive, lively, noisy  8 |
| rénjiā | 人家 | N [colloq.] the other person, other people; a 3rd person or the speaker himself/herself)  6 |
| rènwéi | 認爲/认为 | EV to think that..., believe that...  5 |
| rèqíng | 熱情/热情 | ADJ warm-hearted, friendly  5 |
| rìqī | 日期 | N date  2 |
| rìzi | 日子 | N (special) day(birthday, anniversary, etc.)  8 |

## S:

| | | |
|---|---|---|
| shǎ | 傻 | ADJ silly, foolish  1 |
| shàng//bān | 上班 | VO to go to work,  to work (in one's office)  9 |
| shāngdiàn | 商 | N store  7 |
| shāngliang | 商量 | V to talk over (for a solution)  7 |
| shàngmiàn | 上面 | PW on top of, on, above  (syn. 上頭,上邊)；  2 |
| shāng//xīn | 傷心/伤心 | VO/ADJ to hurt feelings; sad, heartbroken  6 |
| shāngyè | 商業/商业 | N business, commerce  9 |
| shǎo | 少 | V to lack, be short of  1 |
| shāoděng | 稍等 | PH "One moment,please" "I'll be with you shortly", "Hold on"  6 |
| shāowēi | 稍微 | A slightly (can be shortened as稍    9 |
| shēng//bìng | 生病 | VO to fall ill, get sick  4 |
| shēnqǐng | 申請/申请 | V/N to apply (for); application  1 |
| shí | 時/时 | TW o'clock  (formal use of 點鐘)  8 |
| shǐ | 使 | V to make (sb/sth.)..., cause (sb. to VP) (syn. of 讓)  7 |
| -shì | -式 | BF –style  7 |

| | | |
|---|---|---|
| shìchǎng | 市場/市场 | N market  9 |
| shípǐn | 食品 | N food  8 |
| shítáng | 食堂 | N cafeteria (of a school, hospital, etc.)  5 |
| shìyìng | 適應/适应 | V/ADJ to get adjusted to; accustomed to  4 |
| shòu | 受 | V/CV to receive; by (see Structural Focus)  8 |
| shōudào | 收到 | RV to receive [mail, gift, etc.]  5 |
| shòuhuòyuán | 售貨員/售货员 | N store clerk, salesperson  8 |
| shōushi | 收拾 | V to put (things) in order, tidy up  1 |
| shóuxi/shúxi | 熟悉 | V/ADJ to be/become quite familiar (with), know sth. or sb. well; acquainted with  3 |
| shǔ | 數/数 | V to count (numbers etc.)  6 |
| shuǐdiànfèi | 水電費/水电费 | N utility cost ("water and electricity fee")  7 |
| shuǐtǔ bù fú | 水土不服 | PH negative physical reactions caused by a new environment ("The water and soil don't agree with you.")  4 |
| shùnlì | 順利/顺利 | ADJ/A (progress of a matter) smooth; smoothly, without a hitch  5 |
| shuōbudìng | 說不定/说不定 | MA maybe, perhaps  3 |
| shūxiě | 書寫/书写 | N [formal]  writing (skill)  9 |
| shùyǔ | 術語/术语 | N professional terminology, jargon  9 |
| sījī | 司機/司机 | N chauffeur, driver  2 |
| suàn | 算 | V to count; to be considered as  4 |
| suànle | 算了 | IE "Forget it." "Never mind."  6 |
| suíbiàn | 隨便/随便 | ADJ/A casual, informal; do as one pleases; randomly, casually; carelessly  3 |
| sùshè | 宿舍 | N dormitory, dorm-room  5 |

## T:

| | | |
|---|---|---|
| tàidu | 態度/态度 | N attitude  5 |
| Táiwān | 台灣/台湾 | PW Taiwan  3 |
| tàng | 燙 | ADJ be scalding hot, hotter than normal  4 |
| tán liàn'ài | 談戀愛/谈恋爱 | VO to get romantically involved, to date  3 |
| tào | 套 | M set of (furniture, books, etc.); suit (of clothing, etc.)  7 |
| téng | 疼 | V (a body part) to ache, hurt, pain  4 |
| tián | 甜 | ADJ sweet  8 |
| tiáojiàn | 條件/条件 | N condition, term  4 |
| tiào//wǔ | 跳舞 | VO to dance  8 |
| tīng | 廳/厅 | N hall, parlor  7 |
| tíng | 停 | V to stop  5 |
| tǐwēn | 體溫/体温 | N body temperature  4 |

| | | | |
|---|---|---|---|
| tōng | 通 | V get through (on telephone) | 6 |
| tóngwū | 同屋 | N room-mate (in Taiwan: 室友) | 5 |
| tóngxué | 同學/同学 | N classmate, fellow student (同, "same" prefixed to nouns) | 2 |
| tǔ | 吐 | V to spit, spit something out | 4 |
| tù | 吐 | V to vomit, throw up | 4 |
| tuánjù | 團聚/团聚 | V to get together, reunite | 8 |
| tuántuán zhuàn | 團團轉/团团转 | ADJ (so busy that you) run around in circles | 1 |
| tuījiàn | 推薦/推荐 | V/N to recommend; recommendation | 8 |
| tuīxiāo | 推銷/推销 | V to (promote and) sell, to market | 9 |
| tūrán | 突然 | MA/ADJ suddenly, abruptly; abrupt | 2 |

**W:**

| | | | |
|---|---|---|---|
| wǎng | 往 | CV toward, to, in the direction of | 7 |
| wǎnhuì | 晚會/晚会 | N evening party | 8 |
| wèi...(ér)... | 爲...(而)/为...(而) | CV-A. for (the sake/purpose of...) [therefore]... | 3 |
| wéi/wèi | 喂 | INTERJ Hello! (mostly used on the phone) | 6 |
| wèishēng | 衛生/卫生 | SV/N sanitary; sanitation; hygienic, hygiene | 4 |
| Wú Hǎilín | 吳海琳/吴海琳 | N (Chinese name of) Helen Wu | 1 |

**X:**

| | | | |
|---|---|---|---|
| xǐ | 洗 | V to wash | 4 |
| xī | 吸 | V inhale | 4 |
| xì | 系 | N department (in a college) | 8 |
| xián | 鹹/咸 | ADJ salty | 8 |
| xiàng | 向 | CV toward, to | 2 |
| xiàng(zi) | 巷(子) | N alley, narrow street | 7 |
| xiǎngniàn | 想念 | V [formal] to miss, long for | 8 |
| xiāngxìn | 相信 | V to believe | 2 |
| xiāo | 削 | V to scrape, peel, pare | 4 |
| xiǎoshí | 小時/小时 | N. hour (syn. of 鐘頭) | 6 |
| xībù | 西部 | N the west; western part | 1 |
| xiè dù(zi) | 瀉肚(子)/泻肚(子) | VO [colloq.] to have diarrhea (肚子, stomach, belly) | 4 |
| xíguàn | 習慣/习惯 | V/N to get used to; habit | 1 |
| xíguàn | 習慣/习惯 | N/V habit(s); get in the habit of, be accustomed to;(-guan,-慣, RVE be accustomed to / be in the habit of ...; (吃慣了,睡慣了) | 5 |
| xìnfēng | 信封 | N envelope | 5 |
| xīngfèn | 興奮/兴奋 | ADJ/N excited, thrilled; excitement | 1 |

| | | |
|---|---|---|
| xìngqíng | 性情 | N disposition  5 |
| xìngqù | 興趣/兴趣 | N interest (in sth.)  9 |
| xīnkǔ | 辛苦 | ADJ/N laborious, toilsome; toil  2 |
| xīnshuǐ | 薪水 | N salary  9 |
| xīnxiān | 新鮮/新鲜 | ADJ fresh  4 |
| xìnxīn | 信心 | N confidence, faith  9 |
| xīyān | 吸煙/吸烟 | VO to smoke (cigarette or cigar)  7 |
| xuélì | 學歷/学历 | N educational background  8 |
| xùnliàn | 訓練/训练 | V/N to train; training  9 |
| xūyào | 需要 | V/N to need; needs  9 |

## Y:

| | | |
|---|---|---|
| yà | 亞/亚 | Asia (used as suffix, but also as prefix (亞洲, Yàzhōu, Asia)  3 |
| Yàkě | 亞可/亚可 | N (one common transliteration for 'Jacques')  2 |
| Yǎkè | 雅克 | N (another common transliteration for 'Jacques')  2 |
| Yáng | 楊/杨 | N (a Chinese surname)  7 |
| yángé | 嚴格/严格 | ADJ strict, harsh  (can be shortened to 嚴)  5 |
| yàngzi | 樣子/样子 | N appearance, look  1 |
| yàofāng | 藥方/药方 | N prescription  4 |
| yàojǐn | 要緊/要紧 | ADJ urgent, important  5 |
| yāoqǐng | 邀請/邀请 | V/N to invite; invitation  8 |
| yèwù | 業務/业务 | N business activities, field stuff  9 |
| yī | 醫/医 | V to treat (a patient, an ailment);BF medical  4 |
| yì | -裔 | BF of descent  1 |
| yìbān | 一般 | ADJ general, average, run of the mill  6 |
| yílù shùnfēng | 一路順風/一路顺风 | PH "Bon voyage!" "Have a nice trip!"  1 |
| yímín | 移民 | V/N to immigrate/emigrate; immigrant/emigrant  1 |
| yínháng | 銀行/银行 | N bank  7 |
| yǐnliào | 飲料/饮料 | N beverage  8 |
| yíqiè | 一切 | N all; everything  5 |
| yīshēng(zhōng) | 一生(中) | N a life-time; all/throughout one's life  3 |
| yīshēng | 醫生/医生 | N (medical) doctor, physician  4 |
| yīwùshì | 醫務室/医务室 | N clinic, medical office (of a school, company)  4 |
| yóu | 油 | ADJ/N oily, greasy; oil, grease  8 |
| yóujú | 郵局/邮局 | N post office  7 |
| yǔ | -語/-语 | BF language, speech (used as N-suf)  1 |

| yuǎn | 遠/远 | ADJ far  2 |
| yuányīn | 原因 | N reason, cause  3 |
| yuē | 約/约 | V to make an appointment  1 |
| yuèdú | 閱讀/阅读 | V/N. to read; reading  9 |
| yuēhǎo | 約好/约好 | RV to fix time/place, etc. for a meeting  1 |
| yuèliang | 月亮 | N the moon  8 |
| yuè xīn | 月薪 | N monthly salary  9 |
| yúshì | 於是/于是 | CONJ so, then, thereupon, therefore  9 |
| yùshì | 浴室 | N bathroom (with or without toilet)  7 |

## Z:

| zhāng zuǐ | 張嘴/张嘴 | VO to open the mouth  4 |
| zhàn xiàn | 佔線/占线 | VO [of phone line] be busy, occupied  6 |
| zhāojí | 着急 | V/ADJ to worry; be worried  6 |
| zháo liáng | 着涼/着凉 | VO to catch cold  4 |
| zhǎo//qián | 找錢/找钱 | VO to give change  8 |
| zhènghǎo | 正好 | A/MA just at the right time; just right; coinci dentally, it just so happens that  3 |
| zhèngmíng | 證明/证明 | V/N to prove, certify; certifying letter  4 |
| zhěngqí | 整齊/整齐 | SV neat, orderly  7 |
| zhēn yàomìng | 真要命 | IE It's awful! It drives me crazy!  4 |
| zhíwù | 職務/职务 | N (job) position  9 |
| zhǐyào | 只要 | MA as long as  (often used with 就）  7 |
| zhǒng | 種/种 | M type, kind  1 |
| zhōngqiūjié | 中秋節/中秋节 | N The Moon Festival (lit. "mid-autumn festival"  (15th day of the 8th lunar month))  8 |
| zhōngshì | 中式 | MOD Chinese-styled (e.g.,中式傢具）   7 |
| zhòngshì | 重視/重视 | V to regard as important, take sth. Seriously  5 |
| zhōngxīn | 中心 | N center  2 |
| zhù | 祝 | V to wish (as in "I wish you luck")  1 |
| zhuǎn | 轉/转 | V to foward, transfer; (envelope) care of (c/o)  5 |
| zhùlǐ | 助理 | N assistant  9 |
| zhǔnbèi | 準備/准备 | V/N to prepare; preparation  1 |
| zhǔxiū | 主修 | V/N to major (in); major (in college)  3 |
| zhǔyào | 主要 | MOD/A main, major, essential; mainly, essentially  9 |
| zhúyì | 主意 | N [colloq] idea  6 |
| zhùyì | 注意 | V to pay attention to, watch  4 |

| | | |
|---|---|---|
| zìcóng | 自從/自从 | MA (ever) since  6 |
| zìdiǎn | 字典 | N dictionary  9 |
| zìláishuǐ | 自來水/自来水 | N tap water  4 |
| zìrán | 自然 | ADJ/A natural; naturally  1 |
| zì yǐ wéi shì | 自以為是/自以为是 | PH to regard oneself as right; disregard the opinions of others  3 |
| zǒngsuàn | 總算/总算 | MA at long last, finally (for 總  )  2 |
| zū | 租 | V to rent  7 |
| zuì | 醉 | V to get drunk; drunk  8 |
| zuò | 做 | V to be (a teacher, manager, mother , etc.)  9 |